In Defense
of the
Psychological

by John William Miller

The Paradox of Cause
The Definition of the Thing
The Philosophy of History
The Midworld
In Defense of the Psychological

In Defense
of the
Psychological

John William Miller

W · W · Norton & Company
NEW YORK   LONDON

The essay "History and Case History" appeared, in somewhat shortened form, in *The American Scholar* for spring 1980, copyright © 1980 by the United Chapters of Phi Beta Kappa. It is reprinted here with permission.

Published simultaneously in Canada by George J. McLeod Limited, Toronto.
PRINTED IN THE UNITED STATES OF AMERICA.
The text of this book is composed in 10/12 Bembo, with
display type set in Bulmer.
Manufacturing by The Maple-Vail Book Manufacturing Group.

FIRST EDITION

Library of Congress Cataloging in Publication Data

Miller, John William.
    In defense of the psychological.

    1. Psychology—Philosophy.   2. Psychology,
Pathological—Philosophy.   I. Title.
BF38.M54   1983   150'.1   82–10566

W. W. Norton & Company, Inc.,
500 Fifth Avenue, New York, N.Y. 10110
W. W. Norton & Company Ltd.,
37 Great Russell Street, London WC1B 3NU

                1 2 3 4 5 6 7 8 9 0
        ISBN 0-393-01701-X

Contents

Preface

One thing I would propose to avoid in presentation of human nature is any over-all impression that mental life has an environment. The basic reason for that is the long existence of skepticism. That insight antedates Freud by a good bit.

And I feel sure that man must be seen as the rational animal, as Aristotle said. Consequently, I hold that all illness of mind is a departure from rationality.

It follows that no one will understand illness who does not understand the mind in its rational ideal. Self-control, that is, freedom, is the essence of psychology, or else psychology disappears. There is no psyche in the determinate. These are radical issues and cannot be evaded. Modern psychology books are written from the slant of determinism, whether a materialist or a psychic sort.

What intrigues me in the concept of "learning" is the impossibility of defining an act without reason. Reason, however, has been sometimes seen as "rationalization," and for the rest as a result of nonrational urges. A very recent but still pre-Freudian statement of this view occurs in the preface to the first edition of F. H. Bradley's *Appearance and Reality* (1893): "Metaphysics is the finding of bad reasons for what we believe upon instinct, but to find those reasons is no less an instinct."

But reason is not modification of original nonreasonable urges or instinct. It is not true, I believe, that reason is the modification of instinct by learning. It is, rather, the case that instinct is itself defined only as the nonrational factor in the life of reason. Strictly speaking, instinct never operates in man. I do not mean that it operates in a *modified* form, but strictly that it *never* operates. Instinct operates in animals. It is precisely the mark of mind, that is, of reason, that instinct is idealized. There is no reason for eating; but eating is a mode of reason, an activity known to contribute to nature and to self. Sex is a mode of reason. One is a dunce to approve of sex, or to disapprove of it. But one is a dunce, too, for approving or disapproving of the multiplication table.

I will admit to no case of instinct that is not, thus, the literal vehicle of the life of reason. I will not admit that reason is revision of instinct. I will not admit that learning disguises instinct. Rather, I hold that learning and reason are necessary conditions for discerning instinct. I would like to see either Watson or Freud define an *act*. Neither does. Neither can. And I know why. The reason is that both want to begin with the facts, but with facts not already colored by reason.

The normal, in a word, is the conditions of action. From that point of view one can explain medical psychology.

For example, libido cancels action. It is no instinct. It is the name for one element in action (pleasure) made inorganic and absolute. But that is nothing new or Freudian. I cannot in all conscience see Freud's work as peculiarly original on that point. Then, for another example, anxiety is the natural *result* of a division in the self, as when one worries over one's status in the community. One needs no "conscience" or "superego" to understand that. Anxiety comes as a sign that one has ceased to define oneself through the community. Its source is ethical. Anxiety is always the sign of a breach in the integrity of the self in some *systematic* way. And that is an old story too. Circumstance never breeds a pathological anxiety; it only affords the occasion for revealing some lack of integrity.

I really would like to find out what is new in medical psychology. The more I look at it, the more I feel that the only part of it that has puzzled me is its theory, not the phenomena it observes. And I do not think its theory is correct. It comes with a scientific authority. And that, I think, is what made it persuasive and acceptable. But I must confess to a dull sense of disbelief and helplessness over any theory of man that does not give critical faculties the primary authority. Only they can fail. There is no failure in biology, no sickness even. There can be pain, but no unhappiness. For unhappiness means a falling out with oneself.

It is health that defines illness, not illness health.

One can't get ahead of oneself in any problem of human nature. No student of human nature is in charge of his own account so long as he employs theories in any way external to his direct experience. Every term used must be meaningful only as a structure-factor in one's own life, never as an object in a region not defined in experience itself. That matters of quality (sensation) and also objects (perception) fall within experience seems pretty well allowed by all hands. But that *the way of telling stories*— the structures of our buildings—must also be made of nothing but experience is harder to seize upon. The reason psychiatric conflict is of prime importance is that it is the occasion for the discovery of structures. It reveals how one is put together, the systematic place occupied by the equation between the personality and some actual finite attachment. There I find a prime ingredient of sanity and of reality.

I feel that for anyone who has traces of egoism, the traditional thought-world is sure to make trouble. Either God or nature does away with me. To be an actual person has become nonsense. And I think that is one reason why the American stage has so many clowns. Burlesque serves notice that one isn't taking egoism seriously. But this is an inherently frustrating situation. Some people take to ideas. Others take to violence. What is there open to a contemporary man but ideas or violence? Both are diseases.

Enjoyment has become fantastically difficult. For example, parents no longer enjoy children. If "intelligent" and "educated," they must "train" the child. He becomes a problem and a pest. Nobody but the yokel, it seems, can close with life and taste it. Thought has become a malady, instead of a delight. This is due to the current frame of reference of thought, namely the inhuman. I say that the frame is our own and that our egoism can secure reality in thought itself. This is heresy. But I do think it is a heresy to which psychiatry gives support, as it helps to reveal that the ego finds itself in the superego, the self in the integrity of the dynamic conditions of conflict.

1

What Is Psychology?

It is always hard to tell what any study investigates. Suppose one says that psychology studies the various mental functionings that appear in many lists. None of these terms or names indicates an object. There is no *object* that is a memory or an emotion.

This should not be too alarming. There is no object that is a number or a triangle or a cause or an error. We constantly use words that do not indicate a particular object or sort of object. All science studies some abstract element in experience rather than some specific object. Sciences are concerned with the form or shape of experience rather than with its specific content. Science studies organization, or the modes of organization. Each subject studied or listed in a college catalogue is about one of the ways of organization. The same objects that are counted in arithmetic are weighed in physics and combined in chemistry. They are bought and sold. They are used for the arts, as in building, painting, making music. A science studies some aspect of the organization of objects, or some peculiar way of acting upon them.

Psychology has no objects different from those of arithmetic or physics or literature. The objects are the same. But psychology examines a peculiar way of organizing such objects, a peculiar set of relations into which they fall.

If one counts the trees on the north side of Main Street, one employs arithmetic. Objects are related that way. If one paints a picture of the trees, one is an artist. If one burns some wood from the trees, one is a chemist. If one remembers that the trees have grown in the last ten years, one is a psychologist. Trees can be counted, painted, burned, and remembered. Trees permit, and even require, a variety of ways of entering experience and of being acted upon.

Now, most people would allow that it is not possible to pass an examination in chemistry by counting trees. Chemistry can't be reduced to arithmetic. Something new has been added. One can't say that psychology is "nothing but" chemistry, that it can be "reduced" to chemistry or to physics, whether mechanics or electronics. If one remembers a tree, one does not therefore know about biology, or combustion, or square root.

There is a strong disposition to deny this. Remembering, perceiving, feeling, are often claimed to be "nothing but" chemical change or physical change. So, too, it is sometimes said that biology is only a vague chemistry or physics, or physics a vague mathematics. It is not easy to show that one sort of experience is not reducible to another. In some cases, not too much is known about the nature of a special study. Is economics part of psychology, or history a part of biology? Or are they all aspects of theology? Some say so.

The only way to settle this question—the question whether one science reduces to another—is to try to tell the story of the supposed basic science without using any word or operation derived from the other. Could you, for example, tell the story of biology using only the words of a physics or chemistry text? Do the words and ideas of physics suggest the problems of biology? Again, do the words and problems of biology suggest the words and problems of psychology?

Suppose one wants to know why one finds it easier to remember the date of Pearl Harbor than the date of the firing on Fort Sumter. Would that question occur in physics? In chemistry? In biology? Suppose one wants to know why Lady Macbeth walked in her sleep. Would one dis-

cover the answer by using yardsticks or clocks or amme-
ters? Does a yardstick give you a clue to a person called
Lady Macbeth? Where does one acquire such problems and
ideas?

The psychological aspect of experience seems at least as
direct and immediate as the arithmetical or chemical or historical. The memories, illusions, madnesses, emotions, and
hungers of experience seem no more strange and no less
original than the quantities or energies of objects. Fear, love,
hate, anger, all seem no more obscure and no less original
than genera and species, or the chemical elements.

Psychology is concerned with those properties of our
experience that make for individuality. Psychology studies
the fact that other experiences occur in particular ways and
in particular persons. That I now remember a tree is as
close and important an element in my experience as the
location of the tree, its species, height, specific gravity, and
the rest.

Psychology is the order of the personal, the form of
individuality. General psychology is the psychology of
learning or of purpose. Abnormal psychology is the psychology of self-revision.

Only specific acts are relevant. Sensation, perception, and
so forth, are incidental factors—or contributing factors—
in purpose. Here one discovers capacities, sensory equip-
ment, interests, and such. Here one also explains specific
reactions (or actions) through prior experience, such as
training. Thus, one can understand a person's preferences
in food, dress, amusements, and the like. One does this by
learning about his opportunities, his habits and those of his
groups, his successes and failures.

This is the region of manipulation, as in advertising, in
rewards, and so on. What inducements one can offer vary
with the learned facts and with the practical values of the
activity in which a person is engaged. Thus, the clothing a
person will buy varies with climate, occupation, and general social situation. In the country one thing, in the city
another. Yet this manipulation has limits, namely those of

a person's knowledge and activity. A very good salesman could not sell an urban executive a pair of overalls, or a farmer a cutaway, or a carpenter a spike when he needs a tack.

The first postulate of general psychology is: *Every act is specific.* The understanding of an act occurs in terms of laws that define the specific. Thus, peculiar knowledge is presumed in a peculiar act, peculiar interests, feelings, and so on. And every case of knowledge, memory, feeling, and the like, is peculiar. That one believes so-and-so, rather than something else, is due to peculiar experiences, that is, to experiences that are themselves to be defined only as items in a unique and individual sequence.

A second postulate in general psychology is: *The specific act has no objective necessity.* It has no nonpsychological environment to which the act is to be referred for its origin and comprehension. This means that an act, or any part of it, such as perception or memory, must be understood only through past experience and not through "facts" viewed as nonpsychological, or as no part of actual experience. The laws of the act describe the occurrence of the unique. They are the form of the unique or individual.

The act is neither merely typical (physics) nor yet chaotic (indeterminism). Psychology depends on the category of the lawfully individual. Its explanations are of the form "You do this because you are so-and-so." They are not of the form "You do this because nature is so-and-so." The act discloses the content of nature; it does not disclose the abstract appearance of an abstract and impersonal fact. Psychology says, "You do so-and-so because it *seems* to you that the situation is thus-and-so." Thus, the act is the revelation of appearance.

That there is appearance can be discovered only through the act. In passivity there is no appearance. Neither is there reality. Reality is the assertion of appearance in an act. An act says, "It seems to me." Psychology studies the aspect of reality that is its appearance, and the act as explained by appearance.

The psychology of self-revision, or abnormal psychology, studies the act as explained by reality. It emphasizes the person, who also possesses appearances, but it deals not with the appearances but with the person. Thus, general psychology says that one remembers the hurricane of 1938 because one saw it, and because some present incident serves to recall it, and because one was impressed by its power at the time. But abnormal psychology says that one remembers it because its violence unsettled one's nerves, challenging one's steadiness or one's confidence or one's ability to cope with situations, or because it brought a moment of sadistic abandon, of release and dissolution. These sources of memory refer to the person, not to the appearances. Abnormal psychology deals with acts expressive of a disordered view of the agent, or of the self, that is, of the reality in an act, not of the appearance in an act. Thus, an act in general psychology is modified by new appearances; in abnormal psychology by a new reality.

2

Grades of Organic Activity:

Physiology	*General Psychology*	
UNCONSCIOUSNESS	CONSCIOUSNESS	UNCRITICAL REASON
Reflexes	Instinct	Thought and action within the limits of uncritical structure
Autonomic	Nature as consciousness	
No learning		
Neither appearance nor reality	Learning as habit	Common sense
	The "healthy" animal	Instinct modified by idealization
	Appearance without reality	The "healthy" human
		Appearance and reality uncritically distinguished

the Locus of the Abnormal

The Normative PURE REASON	The Abnormal IRRATIONALITY	The Normal RATIONALITY
Formalism Pure Order The "bloodless categories" Logic Ethics Math Physics Idealization without instinct *Reality without appearance*	Conflict of instinct idealized, with the demands of that idealized form, i.e., of uncritical reason with pure reason Incompatible idealizations of instinct (Libido = shrinking from normative; ego = shrinking from instinct) Failure of instinct, common sense, and criticism *Confusion of appearance and reality*	Return to instinct and to the normative as the order of instinct Integration The true organism Autonomy in the union of instinct, common sense, and the normative *Self-conscious distinction of appearance and reality*

Remarks

If this map has any merit, it lies in the use made of the normative as a factor in the location and definition of the abnormal and the normal.

In teaching general psychology I found myself forced to ascribe a type of control not derived from instinct. All the books are weak here. This type of control is the idealization of instinct—instinct interpreted in some view of man and nature. Call it "social heredity," although that is clearly not quite the term. For man, instinct has "meaning." It must have meaning in order to permit its discovery, and the assessment of its force.

Instinct by itself produces no conflict. It is only human forms of instinct that can generate conflict, that is, idealized forms, some "common sense" view of instinct. But in common sense, instinct is already objectified. Consequently there will occur the problem of its *proper* interpretation in one's common sense. Thus, common sense breaks down. This leads first to a generalized formulation of its laws, say to the discovery of logic and ethics—the normative. When these reinforce common sense, as they are usually made to do, no abnormality can occur. But when formalism is in any way brought to the surface—when one becomes aware of its claims—one finds that common sense is a mess of confusion, that it veils various and irreconciled demands. It will veil, for example, libido and morality, or filial impulses and egoistic impulses, and so forth. Its idealizations are confused, uncritical, even undefined, yet felt. There would be no conflict without common sense. But what makes common sense confused is the incoherence of its idealizations.

The instincts of general psychology could never generate conflict. They mark success and failure in purposes, never the division of the self. Abnormal psychology marks no defeat of any particular purpose. It marks the inability of an instinctive purpose to prove satisfactory *even when it reaches its specific goal.* In terms of general psychology such a frustration is a contradiction, an absurdity.

The normative here stands for any form of abstract idealization. More particularly, it stands for the evaluation and control of instinctive or impulsive acts. It stands for the law and *the abstractly objective*.

The abnormal then is defined as the stage of development where instinct and norm confront and cancel each other. This results in the flight to subjectivity, or in the flight to an egoism devoid of spontancity, as in fanaticism and aggression of all sorts. The subjective flight corresponds roughly with libido, passivity.

Thus, the map implies the denial that libido and aggression are "instinctual drives." It implies that the only instinctual drives are those of general psychology, namely, the *activity* that assimilates nature to purpose.

It implies, too, that general psychology deals with the *satisfaction* of purposes; abnormal psychology, with the *order* of purposes, their idealization, their relevance to the self, their place in the self, and their meaning for the self. Thus, no one quite knows whether his idealization (theoretical view) of sex—the sex of general psychology—stands for the meaning of sex in the self. It is apropos of the latter that conflict arises. Sex as purpose or as instinct is only a practical problem, never a medical problem.

The normative has always had a hard time of it. It has tended to be viewed as without foundation in instinct and, hence, in learning. Here it stands merely for a necessary condition of the recognition of the instinctual. Where the normative is absent (animals), instinct is only consciousness. The normative is a condition for the identification of the psychological (instinct, learning).

Conflict—the abnormal—is always a sign of the failure to assimilate instinct to norms. The norm appears as "reality," to which the instinct must get "adjusted." This reality is called physical and social. But such ideas are not environmental *objects;* they name the discovery of environment in principle, and so they name noninstinctual elements of action. It is through these noninstinctual factors of action that action becomes confused and blocked.

Instinct must have the environment, which negates it.

There, is the general locus of conflict, the generic schism of the self apropos of which all the various types of malady occur.

The confusion in books on abnormal psychology derives from the scouting of the instincts of general psychology and the substitution of secondary and derived attitudes such as libido and ego. Such attitudes are without exception parasitic. *They do not generate nature.* They do not define learning. They *assume* a consciousness and its objects that they cannot define. As a result, the pedagogy of abnormal psychology becomes irrelevant to general psychology, to the bewilderment of the student.

Psychiatry, in trying to be "scientific," tries to remain "objective," that is, to tell a story in terms of consciousness. Yet *no* idea of abnormal psychology is an idea of consciousness. On the other side, no idea of general psychology generates conflict. There is the impasse.

Thus, in terms of this map, abnormal psychology becomes a theory of the function of general psychology, namely a theory of the role of instinct. *Within* general psychology, instinct has no theoretical function. It is datum and original energy, nothing more. But in abnormal psychology, instinct itself is brought into question, and so also the region of objects that instinct defines and then negates.

In sum, I would say that general psychology deals with purpose, and abnormal psychology with will, that is, with the order of purposes. But the order of purposes can never be suggested or revealed apart from the medium in which purposes operate, namely nature (physical and social).

Thus, abnormal psychology reveals nature as a polar factor of self-consciousness, never as object. Scientific abnormal psychology treats nature as object and thus misses the necessary condition of a conflict. So, too, one wonders whether or not madness is an episode in the "learning" process. It is so presented. And that, I hold, is impossible.

Liability to madness is proportional to the amount and rate of change of the normative (or objective) factors in a culture. Specific madness always reflects that specific cultural norm. *But that culture must be one's own.* I am not made mad by the norms of the Afghans. One's own norms prove troublesome *not* because they are current in one's *neighborhood,* but because one's impulses are idealized in them. Were madness a problem of consciousness only, this would not be the case. No instinctive need, as yet unidealized, can occasion conflict or generate abnormality. No external "reality" can do that. But "reality" can and does bring about madness, because "reality" is only the name for the order of nature in which instinct operates, an order never given apart from the instinct or with any meaning apart from it. On the other side, neither is the instinct identifiable without that order.

Thus, the abnormal becomes a necessary stage in the attainment of normality. But there is neither normality nor abnormality in objects.

Our ills are generated by a mistrust of those instincts that secure access to nature. We can't *act,* because we are forced to mistrust impulses and can't certify them, sometimes in detail, sometimes in principle. The madman can't *act.* He has no control, lacking either impulse or norms.

This map is not complete. I do feel that it is so far so good and not to be cut down. I see other problems of classification and genesis, but I think they can be given a place in this context.

3

The Genesis of the Psychological

In ancient times the psychological was "opinion," in contrast with knowledge: appearance *vs.* the real, or *vs.* the true, or *vs.* the constitutional, or *vs.* the formal. This was not a contrast of "mental" with some absence of mind. *Both* appearance *and* its opposites were psychic. In any case, the psychological was never without some contrast with the nonpsychological, even though the nonpsychological might be "mental."

However one is to come upon an event called "psychological," it will be an event sharing a *common quality* with the nonpsychological. For example, even in the case of seeing and tasting, we say that each is a "sensory" process or that red and sweet are "sense data." What common quality can be shared by the psychological and the nonpsychological? The ancients saw both as "mental," that is, as features of experience. Thus, Plato did not treat geometry as "opinion" or as appearance. For all that, it was "mental," a discipline, universal and formal.

The "mental" was the common denominator of opinion and truth. It seemed that there was no doubt about the mental status of opinion, of appearances. Protagoras had his "opinions." They were his. Each man was the "measure" of all things. But in trying to find something other than opinion, the "mental" status of that other factor was retained. Form, order, constraint, connection were all equally mental, although not the same as opinion.

So the nonpsychological was whatever was *not opinion*.

That what was not opinion was also "mental" expressed no prejudice in favor of the "mental." The nonpsychological appeared as the regular, the organized, the orderly and formal. It appeared as control. Opinion seemed vagrant and hardly mental at all. It was scatter-brained. It was mental only as an incoherent state of mind, not as a thing. Substance or entity denominated a mind. In fact, the trouble with opinion was that it destroyed mind rather than illustrated it.

Appearance, opinion, the psychological, all appeared rather as the *absence* of mind than as its primary evidence. In opinion one had not yet acquired a mind. To have a mind was to discover what was precisely *not* opinion. It was to discover control, to move away from vagrant content, to find order. The first order so found was geometry. To have an intimation of mind was to be a geometer. So Plato.

As opinion, appearance, the stream of consciousness, the manifold of qualities, there was no mind at all. *The psychological was not the mind.*

Today we are still moving away from opinion, from appearance, from the vagrant and disorderly. Just like Plato and Aristotle, we want the nonpsychological. We do not want a world defined by appearance. But it is a historical anachronism to say that in abandoning appearance we are abandoning what was formerly called mental. That is false.

The ancients said that in abandoning appearance we found mind. The modern behaviorist says that we then find *no* mind. But this claim is based on a misconception, namely that mind has been identified as appearance. It was not so. In so far as we equate psychology with opinion, appearance, the manifold, the stream of consciousness, we have not found *either* the mind or—as behaviorism claims—the region of the not-mind. Both ancients and moderns agree that we must get away from psychology.

The question is not whether we move away from psychology; it is, rather, what we have when we have done so. Nobody ever settled for psychology. All agree that until we do get away from psychology, which is only appearance, we are not in the "real." That "real" is not to be psychological. All want to get away from it, Plato no less than B. F. Skinner. The basis of the appeal of Plato and that of B. F. Skinner are identical. But where are we then?

The objection of behaviorism to Plato and others is not that they proposed to get away from psychology but that they arrived at the wrong version of the nonpsychological. The behaviorist feels that those earlier men did not leave mind behind them in getting away from the psychological; instead, the historical fact is that what they left behind was, for them, not mind at all. They said that to find mind, you had to move *away* from psychology. They said, too, that to find the real, you had to move away from psychology. In terms of opinion, or of appearance, one had no mind. In moving away the ancients found mind, but the behaviorist finds not-mind.

The force of ancient criticism was not in preserving the "mental." The force was the search for order, regularity, the nonpsychological, even the nonpersonal. In fact, a problem that developed from the ancient quest for order was the fate of the individual person. They had trouble with it. In getting away from psychology they arrived at a disqualification of the present person as a center apart from, or independent of, the real world. This is exactly what we have in behaviorism. Neither epicureans nor stoics authorized the individual. They "accepted the universe." Local autonomy was *not* the outcome of ancient inquiry into an ordered world. Other examples will serve.

There was, in fact, a positive resistance to local autonomy. In that respect B. F. Skinner says nothing new.

But some account needs to be given of why the psychological ever fell under suspicion, of how it could fall under suspicion. That it did is a matter of recorded testimony. But why? What could possibly have led to the identification of opinion and appearance? What could suggest that attempt to get out of the stream of consciousness? Nothing in it offers a hold for escape. Why not, then, have "consciousness expansion"? (Of course an induced vagrancy is not a consistent idea, on the premises. If we were adrift, we could not produce drift. We could not know that we were there to drift, any more than we would know what to do in order to arrest it or to accelerate it.)

Now, this is a critical point, and there will be disputes over what launched the discovery and criticism of appearance. But whatever we say about it, we have to settle for the fact that it did occur. The account of it should not obliterate the actual event, so voluminously evidenced.

Something nonpsychological must have been familiar if the psychological was to be offset. What was it? What was the source of the assurance that noted the drift of appearance? Where were those men not adrift?

It was in what they did, and in that sort of doing that embodied control. They could count, they could measure, tell distances, times, differences. It was precisely in those terms that the nonpsychological was developed. If you can tell differences, you will end with genera and species, and because you *tell* the differences you will soon be writing a book in logic, which is all about maintaining the capacity to tell differences and not be confused in the telling. Nearer, farther, the way to the port of Miletus, were all very general elements of what one did. How far were you from Miletus? How far offshore was the approaching ship? If you were a bit of a geometer, like Thales, you could tell, and you could say that the distance was "really" more or less than it seemed. You could "prove" it. The appearance stood in contrast with the reality.

Unless the "real" originated in a present assurance it would be no more than another miracle of appearance. That assurance was functioning or actuality. That was the lever that pried appearance and psychology loose from the nonpsychological. This lever was the act; but it was the act, not as a particular, but as a *general form* of acting. It was, indeed, nonindividual. That is what Euclid said to Ptolemy. B. F. Skinner is barking up the wrong tree when he accuses the ancients of not wanting to get rid of psychology or of not finding the nonindividual. They were hot after it, passionately eager. So is he. But he tells no story of how the nonpsychological came to notice. He tells no story of how the psychological fell under suspicion in the first place. As an alternative to psychology, behaviorism has no genesis. It is arbitrary. But the ancients were not arbitrary in *their* discovery.

For the ancients the opposite of appearance was order, and order was the same as mind. This opposition is essential to any assertion of appearance. The result is that Skinner has abandoned appearance. His rejection of a universal order is the consequence of his rejection of psychology. He wants a local control as absolute. But local control made itself evident in action, and in the form of action that projected the universal.

Let us join Skinner in holding out for local control. But let us then recognize how such control was discovered.

4

Knowledge and Psychology

The great *object* of knowledge has tended to be nature. The *test* of knowledge has usually involved logical operations, notably noncontradiction. The *source* of knowledge has tended to be psychology, notably sensation or perception together with other functions such as memory, imagination, interest, attention, and learning. But sensation has a strong position as the chief mode of all empirical knowledge. At a minimum, one is likely to hold that there is no empirical knowledge without it. (I would so hold.)

There is no question, usually, about the relevance of sense qualities in the *extension* of knowledge. An apple is red; if one takes a bite, it may also be sweet or sour. There is no question, usually, about the role of sensation in the *scope* of knowledge. The range of a sense controls what one may know in its terms. Thus, one may or may not hear higher or lower tones. Likewise for color range, taste discrimination, and so forth.

Thus, the presence of sensation, and its role throughout natural knowledge, is likely to lead one to regard it as the *sole* condition of such knowledge. This position gets support from the prima-facie inability to make any statement about objects *except* in terms of sensation. This is the claim of Berkeley. A tulip is what it looks, smells, and feels like, and it is nothing more. It soon develops, however, that no one quality, or group of qualities, is essential for natural knowledge. The deaf man can have objects. So can a blind man. Nor, if one sees, need one possess the entire color range; a color-blind man is not excluded from perceptions. This leads to the result that while quality may be a necessity for our knowledge of nature, this necessity is not based on the necessity of any *particular* quality, and so becomes the necessity of quality in a general or generic sense. *That there be quality* is now what is essential. This suggests that quality has a role to play in experience. To say that is, however, to treat experience as if it were identifiable only if something *more* than quality were present in it. All one can know about an apple is in terms of its qualities, all but one thing, namely that it is an apple and *not* a peach. This *negation* is not a sense quality, yet it is no less necessary than a sense quality if one is to say that apples are sweet. Perhaps peaches too are sweet; but then one has so far not made a difference between apples and peaches. And that difference is unavoidable if one is to talk about apples. Similarly, to say there is a quality "sweet" is to say too that it is *not* "sour," or *not* "middle C," or *not* "violet." Qualities occur only as they are discriminated, only where there is difference, or variety. *No quality is identified in isolation.*

Therefore, an apple is not to be perceived as a wholly passive combination of qualities. Every quality of the apple is also *not* some other, and any combination is also *not* some other, that is, the combination that is a peach. The view of knowledge that holds that objects are combinations of qualities is, therefore, untenable. It is based on the erroneous assumption that qualities are mere data, presented and apprehended without any environment of other constituents of perception. It is this error that underlies the view that an apple is nothing but a combination of qualities, each quality being an absolute and original element of knowledge.

It would, moreover, be odd if knowledge lacked this negative factor. If it did, one could never say that apples were not as juicy, or as sweet, as peaches, or as big as melons. Everything would be what it appeared. There would be no criticism of appearance. Yet knowledge means that mistakes have been avoided. If an apple or anything else is a combination of qualities, then no statement about any such combination could be in error. No alternative statement would be right nor any such statement wrong. No quality or combination would be illusory or hallucinatory or imaginary. Conclusion: there is no knowledge of apples until a mistake has been made and corrected. It is this sense of avoiding mistakes that marks knowledge.

No mistake is made in reporting data. It is all one can do with them. If you say one can be wrong about attributing qualities to apples, then some appeal is made to some factor other than quality. If there is no such appeal, then knowledge equals perception whatever it may be. No criticism is possible. This is Plato's point in the *Theaetetus*.

Even if one does no more than report a sense quality "sweet," one has performed a minimal critical act. For to say sweet is to imply "not sour" or not visual or auditory. It is to allege not only a datum, but a *possibility*, "sweet," and to reject others. Thus, *even sense quality assumes judgment*.

Hence, quality is indeed original and essential; but it is original at a price and not to the exclusion of other original factors. The statement "no knowledge without quality" does not imply that "all knowledge is quality." It may have other factors.

Knowledge, and its correlative, "error," requires that any case of knowledge be *liable to error,* and that the error had been avoided. This *avoidance* is the negative and critical factor. The premise of knowledge is, then, a state of affairs that has avoided possibilities; for example "apples grow on trees," *but* "melons grow on vines." If it grows on a vine, it isn't an apple. Or, "salt contains carbon" or "sugar contains sodium" are statements that can be judged. In our knowledge of nature, an *object* is the factor that permits error. This objective status is the condition of error, that is, of a *subjective* state that corresponds to no object.

The object is a composition of qualities. But it is something more; it is the locus of possibilities, but of *determinate possibilities*. Thus, "apples might grow on vines," but if one regards them as a fruit, one would not regard it as possible that one nets them in the ocean or digs for them in a mine. Quality by itself is an *indeterminate possibility*. Some apples are yellow, and are sweet, but lemons are also yellow, and they are sour. Yellow sets no limits to further quality. Some red roses are fragrant; some are not, and this is no logical disappointment.

Experiment pertains to *objects*. The aim of experiment is to establish determinate possibilities, that is, to *identify* objects (this applies only to "trial and error" experiments, which are psychological, not to experiments in physics, which *always* involve symbols). One learns the difference between wood and stone for purposes of building a fire, or among stones for chipping or grinding tools, or for striking fire, and the like. Objects have *expectations* of a limited sort. Not every thing can follow from "wood," any more than from stone or apples. A pun: an apple is an appeal! But yellow is no appeal to anything. It is just a datum.

5

The World in Its Occasions

One claims either a great deal or else very little for the psychological. It runs away with all experience, or else it is a negligible vagrant needing to be brought to account by physics, logic, ethics, theology. It either devours nature and the supernatural or is devoured by them.

Indeed, the very discovery of the psychological smacks of the illicit. It is the place of "mere" opinion, or prejudice, emotion, impulse. Plato took the sophists as standing for this ungoverned immediacy. The psychological became associated with accident and with malady—logical, moral, or Freudian.

Although the occasion for emphasizing the person and the individual, psychology has never seemed acceptable as the full meaning of the person. The person is in charge of himself, but in his psychological aspect he seems in the charge of what is *not* himself. He is not self-contained in the psychological.

Thus the wheels begin to turn, or, as I would say, the dialectic begins to play. One turns to the impersonal in order to find the "true" person. And so one gets lost, again, in what is *not* the self in its immediacy. Here appear "harmony" with "nature" or submission to God, or a frank acceptance of the stream of consciousness as a finality that is factual and "objective."

All such views do, however, preserve the psychological ghost, even if only as what has to be overcome or dealt with. And this ghost is never exorcised.

The stream no longer flows, and so one has fixations and obsessions. As for Freud, I think that he never makes clear this relation of occasion and situation. Act and learning are not for him environment defining. Madness becomes a state of mind and is not there *also* a state of nature. For nature, "reality," remains aloof and imperturbable. But I know nothing about nature apart from its occasions. This, I think, is sanity. Everybody says "go back to nature." I do not think they can mean it, not, that is, on the idea of "nature" as the imperturbable. So they shunt back to consciousness; and there everything becomes a chaotic mess or a mad fixation.

There is great need to define the psychological, a chief problem of our time. This is really where one becomes concerned with Freud. I know of no way of describing madness apart from nature, and no way of describing nature apart from sane experience. To lose the name of action is to lose nature.

6

The Association of Ideas

Every thought sequence is an association of ideas. It would obviously be impossible to have thoughts without association, juxtaposition, sequence. The association of ideas is not, however, usually taken in this purely descriptive sense. It is taken to mean that meanings, memory, and reasonings are adequately *explained* in terms of association. Association is said to account for these other functions. How and what one remembers, means, perceives, or reasons is thus taken to be a product or result of the order and juxtaposition of ideas as originally presented to the mind. The original order determines subsequent order. Hence this theory makes the following assumptions: (1) there is a mind; (2) it is passive or receptive; (3) some influence plays upon it and gives it content; (4) the order of this content is preserved in subsequent nonperceptual presence to mind of these same ideas.

But many frequent and almost constant associations are irrelevant; for example, a fountain pen is most commonly seen in someone's hand, probably one's own, yet the meaning of this instrument, its definition, and its place in understanding are not usually in terms of that frequent but irrelevant association. The "law" of frequency doesn't hold.

A single association may be more powerful over the imagination than many repetitions. The clang of a fire bell may make one's heart sink because of personal losses through fires; the often-seen popular interest in fires doesn't occur to one.

Spatial contiguity is not the key to memory or imagination. Many ideas do bring up spatial accompaniments, but many do not. Since I have seen Cambridge and Boston, the thought of the former may cause me to remember my early desire to go to Harvard, or it may cause me to remember an athletic victory or defeat at New Haven. Things remembered frequently are spatially contiguous, but the exceptions are so numerous that some basis of selection is necessary.

The same holds true of temporal contiguity. Many associations are temporally contiguous—which is only to be expected inasmuch as all events are temporal. But here again there are many exceptions. It is often more difficult to recall a time series than some logical connection. What temporal sequences one remembers are selected by some other element than their temporal sequence.

Recency, again, requires some further selection. A recent association in space or in time may be far less potent than a remote one. And if more potent, it is so evidently for some reason other than mere recency.

Similarity also is not enough. Seeing two men walking, with a fine dog held in leash by one, I may associate the man with the dog rather than with the more similar companion. The Parthenon looks like the temple to Poseidon at Paestum, but it may remind me of Pericles, a Gothic church, the temple at Karnak. Here, too, similars are often remembered, but evidently because of some property other than their similarity.

Nor is the so-called law of affect an adequate explanation. The unpleasant may make as strong an impression as the pleasant. It is at least as important to remember the unpleasant results of attempts as the pleasant; in fact, unless we do remember them, we may repeat them. In solving a puzzle or problem, we may suddenly be successful but not remember how the success was achieved, while what *not* to do may readily occur as we try again. Sometimes the excitement of trying blots out the clear consciousness of the process by which one has succeeded; for example, in finding one's way along a path, success may be accompanied by knowledge that one could not repeat the performance because landmarks were not noted. In general, what not to do precedes what to do as a guide to success.

The law of affect has, moreover, gone beyond the passive view of the mind and the merely pictorial presentation of ideas. It has introduced a new element of purpose or reaction. It suggests that what we remember, or what we associate in any way, is conditioned by purpose. What is connected is connected by one's interest. Interest is the discriminating element. Of course it always operates on objects similar to others or contiguous in space or sequent in time, rarely or frequently or recently presented. These circumstances of association have all in turn been singled out by psychologists as the basis of association, but they remain merely circumstantial and concomitant rather than causal.

Interest, attention, or purpose are not, however, a complete explanation of the grounds of association. There is a cognitive or logical as well as a motor basis. This cognitive basis lies in the *meaning* of the object or experience. This meaning may place a given idea or object or experience in connection with others greatly dissimilar, scattered in space and time, but forming a system of knowledge logically connected. It is this meaning that decides what circumstantial factors will be taken up into the association. A war may remind me of the winner of a Nobel Peace Prize. Of course, there is an ideal contiguity here, but there is much more, namely a selection of a particular one. A book may remind me of Gutenberg because the book is printed, and printing in its causal development leads to its inventor.

This logical element can then be classified under various heads: cause, result, scientific classification, laws of transformation, and so forth. The logical element is joined by this classification to the purposive element, because objects interest us, that is, appeal to the practical, however defined, because in practice we need to know causes, results, and order of transformation. These are the interesting and important aspects of objects. Such matters as contiguity are in themselves entirely trivial and could never serve as a basis for unification.

The logical element may be otherwise defined thus: the unity of meaning of a system of knowledge of which a given idea is a member is what calls up that system, because the idea *means* that system. Every meaning is *ipso facto* a unification of diversities of appearance. An association, then, never points to something outside of the object as a result or a mechanical or fortuitous juxtaposition; rather, it is the inner meaning of the idea itself, its inherent definition in its widest extent, that governs the association.

7

Instinct

i

Theology, physics, psychology have all sought to embrace the past, in so far as we imagine a past, in some ahistoric priority. At present we meet a widely accepted psychological reduction. An alleged agency is to be "explained" by showing that no agency existed, not really. Two broad methods have appeared in psychology. The one is that by which the psychological reduces to physics, the other falls back on the stream of consciousness. The physics line leads to muscles, tendons, joints, and ductless glands, to neurones, dendrites, synapses, to the central and autonomic nervous system, and so to stimulus and response. The stream of consciousness is forced to treat even the "nervous system" as another content of consciousness.

But even in the common psychology of learning, as well as in the psychology of confession and conflict, there has been a factor neither quite physical nor yet quite the same as another blandly neutral content. This is called "instinct." One reads of "dynamic psychology," a sort of jet propulsion within the passivity of sensory data, a Gulf Stream within the Atlantic Ocean. These instincts—and there have been many lists of them, some longer, some shorter—were also treated as mere phenomena. In the case of medical psychology we no more knew of the lurking drive of sex or aggression than we knew about the appendix or the localization of apparatus in the brain. Sex, of course, is no recent discovery. Venus had long been a mighty power, nothing short of a divinity, both benign and malignant, damaging, energizing, and destructive. But to the empirical and scientific psychologists, any urge, propensity, or instinct appeared as another fact. Were they facts in physics or merely other items in the stream of consciousness? In neither case could they produce an action of one's own. What has been broadly called "science," that is to say, knowledge of any sort, has been based on some mode of order and control. In that sense mathematics is a science, and so is physics or even logic and grammar. But with instincts, whatever list is adopted, we have, allegedly, a scientific idea based on a total lack of control.

ii

Traditional instinct theory is a theory of atomistic urges. There is a specific urge related to a specific type of situation. No general need is, in this sense, instinctive. The general need is only for a maximum of integrity. This can become confused by following specific urges. Specific urges are imperative only as they embody, on a specific occasion, some nonspecific or formally necessary element of personality. For example, when sex is viewed as impulse it can be overcome; but its authority mounts when it is seen to be a chief vehicle of present personal recognition. Then it is no longer instinctive sex but love. Because civilized men cannot follow instinctive sex, and have not been able to give a very trustworthy account of secular love, they are— as men—in conflict between instinct and its control. I suppose that for most men the grounds of such control are lacking. Sex interest becomes subdued by a negation, not controlled by an affirmative grasp of its meaning. All negative check is arbitrary. It is right that there be such arbitrary negative checks. They give an occasion for the understanding of the role of the instinctive urge, its meaning and place in the personal economy. They show the power of the instinct. An impulse that can be checked should be checked. It has no essential or sovereign role. It is scattering, not disorganizing, but merely a preventive of a start toward organization. Social check is thus both a source of difficulty and a source of appreciation. Not to meet it is not to secure a start toward affirmative and self-conscious organization. It is not, then, merely an external fact, but an internal necessity. Check permits the discovery of a general urge, of the truly passionate and affirmative and creative will, the will that has literally found itself through difficulty.

It is right to overcome instinct; it is wrong to overcome nature. Repressive theories confuse this distinction and try to overcome nature. *Instinct refers not to the substance of an urge, but to its status.*

Hence, we are not governed by instinct but by the meaning of instinct in the economy of a total personality. Mere instinct defines brutality. Mere control defines repression, whatever may be the source of the repression. Self-control means that instinct is always more than impulse, and this by the very fact that it is found and identified as impulse. The discovery of instinct is identical with the discovery and experience of conflict. Every identified instinct occurs as an intrusion into some organization of the will and of values. This is the defining and diagnostic mark of an instinctive value. Instinct is not a fact; it is a status in an organized world of value and action. Whatever has power to challenge organization is itself a factor of organization. Nothing else can make that challenge.

iii

Instinct theory is animistic rather than mechanistic.

But animism does not discriminate between instinct and action. It sees all action as natural, as what the living thing is. Aristotle's "entelechy" applied to men and to plants. Their entelechy was their "form," their peculiar mode of activity. It was their essence, their nature. It is the "nature" of the acorn to become an oak, and of man to be rational and a member of society. Animism is only the disclosure of essence. It is teleological in so far as it is for Aristotle a theory of "becoming" or tendency. But the end is not deliberate or purposive or self-conscious. Instinct, however, divides the organism. It denotes the unlearned, not the learned; the spontaneous, not the deliberate; the locus of one's slavery to nature, not one's freedom. Instinct is an idea that has in it some self-consciousness, namely the realization that one is tied to nature, and that one is not a creature of pure thought. Instinct theory is naturalism, but it is a naturalism with a self-conscious element, namely a discovery about oneself, not of a new fact about objects.

Instincts do not define the organism. Instincts tie us to nature, yet they require some separation from nature to permit their discovery and to give that discovery importance, to give it the force of a revelation and of an important fact about human nature.

By looking at living things one would not come by the idea of instinct. There are thousands of insects, fish, birds, higher animals, and plants. Each species has peculiarities. Each has peculiar activities of nutrition, growth, reproduction, and locomotion. It is a bewildering and formless variety that one finds when one merely reports on the activities of all these models of life. All these living things have some career, and all of them do it differently. What, then, would a list of their "instincts" include? It would, of course, include all the mysterious practices of all living things, a glut of mystery indeed. But in all these cases the "instinct" is the animal or plant in its nature or essence. These activities are not separable from them. They have no reserve of soul or personality to which their instincts come as a discovery. They are not alienated from nature but are one with it in all they do. Their life flows in its spontaneity, sometimes calm, sometimes stirred, but always just itself, not threatened by their instinctive nature, not informed or elevated or debased by it.

Life in itself, that is, as any living thing, is not to be

described through instinct. It permits no such difference between itself and its instinctive acts. Of course, it is "conditioned," or it learns. But it learns only in accordance with those activities that define it. It never learns to modify itself, to define itself as not exhausted in its spontaneity. Nor can the observer do more than note positively the actual manifestations of such a life. He cannot separate its instincts from any other aspect. There is no other aspect.

For this reason we do not go to animals and plants to learn what an instinct is. They do not show them. They are what they are, and that is all.

By going only to animals or plants man cannot discover his own specific instincts. Some animals or plants carry out activities similar to ours, but many do not. There is not always bisexuality or the fostering of the young. It is true, however, that where men behave like animals they have found an instinct, even though not all animals or plants may show the same traits.

Still, the fact that an animal is seen to bare his teeth or eat or fight is no more evidence of instinct than the discovery that another man does the same. It is the place of the activity in someone's own life that shows him that nature is in charge, and not himself. It is no factual similarity but the division in oneself that suggests instinct. Not every human being knows he has instincts, and no one can be sure that he has a complete list of his specific modes of attachment to nature. He won't discover his own instincts by observation alone. One would not know what to observe. The experience that one has instincts comes only as some violence is done to one of the modes of our continuity with nature.

iv

Instinct is usually regarded as a native, unlearned, and purposive act. It is represented as an urge to bring about some satisfying result. There is about it both a "drive" and a "goal," or final cause.

One may wonder how an act can be purposive or goal seeking, when at the same time it is said to be unlearned, that is, launched without prevision of the goal, a prevision or foreknowledge that only learning or experience could supply. Goal without foreknowledge seems contradictory. I propose that it is indeed contradictory. I propose that instinct is not purposive. The basis of this proposal is the denial that instinct seeks a goal. To use a simple declarative sentence: instinct seeks no goal. It is contended, further, that neither is instinct vagrant. It is not drift or vagrancy. The combination of these two ideas sets the problem: how can instinct be neither purposive, nor yet drift or vagrancy.

A goal is subordinate to life and experience. It has a "psychic environment." It implements an activity essentially gratuitous. It is an element in the spontaneous functioning of life or action. To eat I must sow and harvest. So I plan to have some corn. That is a goal. It is specific. It falls within the instinctive concern of eating. I might plant beans. I might catch fish or hunt deer. Each is a plan, each is a goal. Each falls within the "psychic environment" of my instinctive activity and, likewise, within the scope of my learning, information, experience, skill.

Instinct, spontaneous activity, is the locus of learning. It opens up the environment of the organism. Learning and environment are correlative terms, that is, mutually implicative. Learning does not assume environment, but generates it. Here one should avoid the fallacy of composition. A specific case of learning does have a pre-established environment, but it does not follow that all learning makes that presumption. Learning in principle has no environment. Nor does learning in principle assume an organism. The difference between organism and environment is generated from learning. It is not, however, a difference among objects in the environment. It is not a distinction among facts or data. It is a reflective and idealized distinction, formal and structural. It is not a logical, but a dialectical distinction.

Instinct, activity, the genesis of environment is not self-preserving or self-assertive. There is no self to preserve until activity has revealed it, and reflection has identified it.

Instinctive activity is neither pleasant nor unpleasant. It has no such intellectual sanction or control. The pleasant and the unpleasant occur within the functioning of instinct. No value judgments can be passed on instinct. Instinct creates the area within which misery and satisfaction occur as episodes. Those episodes are necessary corollaries of spontaneous action, but they are not its control in principle. Here again, as above, it is well to avoid the fallacy of composition.

Plan and vagrancy occur only apropos of instinct. A plan postulates the unquestioned mode of activity it seeks to realize in detail. Vagrancy postulates the activity that is productive of learning and enlarging of control.

Nor is learning, as is sometimes assumed, the answer to a problem or a "problem situation." Problems assume a "productive environment." They are not original, but derivative. Passivity has no problems. Activity generates them. Without original activity no problem has any point. And it should be noted that the problem is not the meaning of activity, is not original, is not the picture of spontaneous action. In spite of its affinity for "radical empiricism," the pragmatic doctrine has an intellectual taint in its premises. That is why the pragmatists fail, at last, to certify enthusiasm, why they look askance at resolve. They are apostles of a dry and pointless intelligence.

On the instinctual level, living has no purpose, not even that of self-preservation. Activity itself is there without worth.

Spontaneity in principle never can be given worth.

Questions occur, however, over the worth of particular instincts. These questions reduce to this: "Is this specific activity (eating, sex) truly spontaneous, that is, a mode of defining the environment and a mode of defining the organism?"

Such questions do not define the environment. They do not lead to learning about the environment. They are questions that take note of action, not of fact. They are reflective questions.

There develops apropos of reflective questions a type of knowledge which is not instinctual, that is, not a matter of learning. All such knowledge marks the discovery that action has occurred. It is knowledge about action itself, or about some ingredient of action.

For example, instinctual consciousness includes identities and differences: this apple and that one; or this apple and that pear; or this woman and that man. Thus it includes quantity. But it does not include mathematics. Mathematics is the knowledge that develops by making quantity its object. More concretely and accurately, it is the generalized story of counting. Counting is grounded in the instinctual fact of differences. But mathematics is the result of making counting (an action) itself the concern of thought.

Again, instinct entails society, as sex, parenthood, gregariousness, and so on. But ethics is a reflection on the activity of being aware of others. It has no denotation in the environment. Like mathematics, it is rather a study of the way one deals with and defines environment. Thus, it, too, is reflective. These considerations show a sort of knowledge not defined within the instinctual, but based on a recognition of act as something already done.

Such knowledge and the activity of getting it has, like instinctual activity, no value. But being self-conscious knowledge, it can certify to the role of instinct. It absorbs instinct into the self. Furthermore, it makes it necessary to accept instinct and is thus therapeutic. And it gives direction to energies because it identifies and certifies the modes of spontaneity. This sort of knowledge can be called "scientific," and in all cases it deals with the shape of spontaneity, never with the objects encountered in instinctual spontaneity. Thus, modern physics becomes a theory of measuring, of seeing, of moving objects from place to place, and so on. Neither mathematics nor physics nor any science deals with the instinctually identified object. It does not deal with "learning," that is, learning how to identify any object or what to do with it. It deals only in shapes, laws, forms, structures. Its vehicle is the symbol, whether the word, a number, a yardstick, clock, or the symbol meaning implication, or the work of art.

This knowledge is the locus of the liberal arts. Science (that is, natural science) becomes the reflection upon the object; the humanities, upon the activities of the organism. The former is the form of the communicated, the latter of communication. But in both cases there is reflection upon something done, never knowledge about the objects or environment of instinct.

I believe that much confusion has been caused by trying to assimilate the reflective to the instinctual sort of knowledge. And much also by trying to separate them. Perhaps most of all, by trying to subordinate instinctual to reflective or "higher" knowledge and activity. On this point I have no opinion. One does not need to have.

Knowledge has direction, then, only if the spontaneity of a directionless instinct be acknowledged. The direction of activity requires the identification and the appropriation of the spontaneous. For example, there is a question whether one needs to learn mathematics or ethics. The answer is dependent upon the acceptance of those instinctive activities that generate environment. A person not wanting to eat and look around and have sexual activity would have no need of mathematics or of ethics.

These remarks are not primarily directed at clarifying reflection but at clarifying instinct. To teach psychology is hard because the books give no sign of understanding the peculiar function of learning—peculiar and limited. When one comes to abnormal psychology it is impossible to generate conflict out of instinctual exploration, and one is left high and dry. The expedient to which abnormal psychology has been driven has been the invention of a new set of instincts, inherently morbid. They are morbid because they do not name the activity by which the environment is defined and discovered. That is a really monstrous error. Consequently they do not and cannot generate the distinction of organism and environment (the self and nature), which is the foundation of all cases and types of conflict.

To use an older expression, instinct generates reason. But this occurs only as the instinctive activity itself comes under notice, only where doing, or some aspect of doing, becomes itself an object of concern, as in counting, measuring, and the like. The objects of reason are not the objects of instinct. That seems to be the result. Instinct itself is the object of reason—an old idea.

Thus, the claim that instinct involves "goals" is a half-truth. It does involve goals, but as the meaning of instinct itself, not as a conscious or unconscious terminus within instinct. He has goals who knows the meaning of his spontaneity. But, by itself, instinct is only activity, satisfactory in itself, with no ulterior end, with no idea of resting from one's labors once one has eaten food or routed an enemy.

v

Can an instinct be sublimated? That is, can an instinct receive alternative, or substitute, expressions?

Instinct means self-defining interest; hence it cannot successfully be turned from its proper expression, its defining expression. To the observer, it may seem that an alleged instinct is being turned into a new channel. But from the inside, the new channel reflects the failure to identify the instinct. From the inside, the apparent sublimation is not a blockage of instinct, but a quite proper manifestation of energy and will.

From the inside, the sublimation might even be denied. The artist might deny that he was sublimating sex. The artist might neglect his family, yet feel no special misgivings. The religious person might forgo sex, yet discover no violation of his will. Why should anyone say to him that his religion is a mark of frustration? Only because the observer has a theory about the necessary forms of personality and its energies. But such a theory could only mark the result of the breakdown of celibacy. It would be a theory that would prove, not sublimation, only that men search for their instincts and do not know them in advance.

Instincts aren't sublimated. They pass through a conflicting mind in order to be discovered. Then, when conflict has been resolved, one is prone to suppose that the instinct has been there all the time, struggling for expression. But that is meaningless. The instinct can't be found or have meaning to anyone apart from the procedure that discovers it.

I propose, therefore, that instead of viewing human nature as already known, we see the area of personal psychology as the story of its discovery. Then sublimation takes on a new meaning. Instead of being an outcome of known forces, it becomes a sign that forces are *not* known, that the clearest channels of energy have not been found. From the inside, the sublimation is an essay at release of energy. From the outside, it seems a blockage of energy, a misapplication, a false expression of a need. But this outside judgment has validity only because the outsider can secure witnesses to the longer output of energy in other ways of acting.

8

Behavior

A "science" of behavior would hardly be suitably named if it had not, like physics and chemistry, exorcised all animistic controls from the changes or events that it proposed to study. Modern science goes its way without invoking the controls associated with purpose, will, or value.

Primitive man was animistic. He found it sensible to associate change with a doing, with his own doing in the first place, and then to attribute the same sort of control to all the objects that touched his own doing, to a spring of water, to wind and waves, to the planets and stars. Any order known to him seemed beyond question of the same sort as the local control directly experienced when he threw a stone or built a fire. He was not aware of an order quite independent of getting what he wanted. He made a little room for himself in a vast apparition. This local order was all the order that came to notice. It does not appear that he saw a chaos around him. There was no opposition of purpose-control to a nonpersonal order or disorder. We now say that primitive man was "animistic," but *he* did not say so. There is no evidence that the distinction of animate and inanimate had been made, while there is a great deal of evidence that the distinction took time and effort to produce. There are still a few primitive tribes, but they do not understand what is meant by the anthropologist who tells them that they are animists. The offset to animism is unknown to them. It is an anachronism to charge them with ignorance, as if they could recognize a defect in a sort of knowledge with which they were now familiar.

The Baconian statement that "knowledge is power" fits the animistic temper as well as that of a Renaissance scientist. Far from now alleging that knowledge is "power," we now regard knowledge as the plain evidence of impotence. We have exorcised purpose-control, which is pragmatic, and will-control, which is historical, from the account we give of nature. This has been considered a great triumph. The triumph of knowledge has reduced us to impotence.

Any intrusion of psychic control is resisted. We are not even allowed to say that every event has a cause. David Hume and Bishop Berkeley saw to that. The attempt of Kant to restore cause and other universals has met heated resistance or contemptuous dismissal. Not only is the purposeful act no longer a basis of order, but judgment itself is denied authority in any story of nature. We had better bite the bullet and stop making a fuss in these declarations of our impotence.

A curious consequence appears in an inability to allege ignorance. Destroy order and you lose any basis for alleging defect. It is today popularly said that "everyone is entitled to his opinion," the reason being that no "title" can be claimed. Title smacks of prejudice and dogma, of limitation, of enforcement, of authority. Even the restraints of logic are repudiated as authoritarian and as menacing us with a "block universe." We ask about "relevance," suggesting that we take mathematics or history on approval. We cannot only do without them, we go further and say that such constraining orders are in violation of free thought, of an open world, of a pluralism, which sets no limits to action or to knowledge. In consequence it is no longer possible to charge ignorance. We cannot say what it is that we do not know. No defect attaches to a lack of acquaintance with mathematics, physics, economics, or history. One does not make a fetish of a tool, and we put anyone who does on the psychiatric couch or lock him up. He has what we call a "fixation."

We do not go quite that far with a person who keeps believing in a causal, quantitative, spatial, and temporal order, but we tolerate such fairly harmless obsessions and may even find them interesting or amusing from an anthropological point of view where any "culture" is another phenomenon, including the propensities of the anthropologist himself.

This is part of the background of "behavioral science," which operates on the premise that, as in physics, purpose-control and will-control are to be exorcised from the phenomena investigated—if one may speak of investigation. But the second string is the repudiation of constraining order of a general sort, even when nonpersonal or nonindividual, as in the rule of cause or in the formulae of physics. For it is not the case that behavioral science falls within the order of physics or chemistry. Indeed, the terms used to describe "behavior" do not appear in physics, where there is no "stimulus" and no "response" but a uniformity of change. A chemical substance is the same as its changes and no stimulus diverts it from its molecular or atomic constitution. Water is liquid, but the liquid can solidify at 32° F and vaporize at 212° F and is identified as water, rather than as alcohol, in such changes. It is the "nature" of water to change in just those ways, and we rely on its identity and remove it from the radiator of an auto when winter comes. There is no hocus-pocus about "conditioning" water to freeze or boil or not to freeze and boil at other temperatures or pressures. Indeed, what would become of the science of physics if by blowing a whistle or ringing a bell fifty times one could make one's morning coffee without the trouble and expense of using wood, coal, gas, or electrical means of agitating its molecules? Why bother with a Bunsen burner in the chemical laboratory? The talents of behavioral scientists should, perhaps, be applied to procuring those "responses" in physics, which would save vast trouble in study and expense. Yet, curiously, nobody proposes to reform physics on behavioral principles. Like physics, behavioral science proposes to exorcise purpose-control or value-control, but unlike physics it proposes no order of change in objects that is the identification, the "nature," of the object. Nature is unconditioned. It looms in its inexorable ways.

The popular appeal of behavioral science rests, in large part, on its attempt to be scientific, that is to say, to do without purpose-control or value-control. But what is not generally noted is that it has no analogy whatsoever with that citadel and rock of science which is physics. A formula such as $S = \frac{1}{2} gt^2$ or $E = MC^2$ is a universal and tells nothing about any event that particularizes its application. It is this that is the majesty of natural science. For a long time there has been controversy over the relation of "body and mind" or "matter and spirit." One solution of the problem was called "parallelism." Nature was seen as going its own way without interference from mind, while mind was represented as the counterpart of nature, unaffected by the forces of laws that defined nature. Each went its own way but on parallel lines that did not intersect. If one went down the street to buy a can of tobacco, the motions of the body received no propulsion or direction from the mind, nor was the state of mind any consequence of the condition of the body. Each factor kept to itself. The law of the "conservation of energy" forbade the intrusion of mind into changes within nature and equally forbade a dissipation of energy in the production of psychic phenomena.

Obviously the supposed radical distinction of body and mind was open to other relations. "Interaction" was warmly advocated. But on the premises of the distinction, it could offer no medium of transition. There was no common ground in so far as the distinction was maintained, no medium neither body nor mind, through which a liaison could operate. And so there were also suggestions of a "reduction" of one term to the other. Bishop Berkeley is noted, or notorious, for his very decent and civil plea to get rid of matter on the appealing ground that nobody ever saw any, a very teasing claim for radical empiricists who want the sensible and true avouch of psychological perception. Others, alleging that they were well acquainted with body or matter, proposed to do away with mind on the quite Berkeleyan ground that mind never appeared and made no difference in their report of objects. For both reductionists it was a complete standoff, each party alleging that it could do very well without the other. This, of course, is familiar ground. But it is a mistake to suppose that the annoying Bishop has been burnt at the stake by scientific orthodoxy. Scientists speak of the collapse of rational order. They say that they tell "how" but never "why." They have no prejudices and are open to all data, not foreclosing the limitless possibilities of experience.

Today there is even discussion over the atom, sub-atom, and sub-sub-atom, whether it exists, whether it is an object or a useful "hypothesis," perhaps a hypothetical object, not an ordinary perceptual object. It is like the famous question of Porphyry about universals, whether they exist or subsist in the bare mind. In any case, the material world is no longer described as an aggregation of sensible objects—not a new discovery. Atoms are an old story and a persistent one.

Behavioral science has not, however, embraced *any* of the traditional relations of body and mind. It is not parallelism; it is not interaction; it is not a reduction of all appearances either to the content of consciousness or to the inexorable uniformities of physical science.

What is the status, then, of the psychologist's pigeon? It occurs neither as an item in a stream of consciousness nor yet, like falling water, in the uniformities of physics, where one cannot tell the scientific difference between a hawk and a handsaw.

And yet it is about as sure as we ever get to be that something there is that changes or "responds" to particular "stimuli." Common objects do not so "respond." They are part of nature as described by physics. There is nothing we can do to change nature's ways. On behaviorist premises, there is no "doing" in any case. Behaviorism is hardly proposing to reestablish an animistic purpose-control. So, one is blocked *both* ways: objects do not respond, and no purpose-control is to be invoked to effect a change in them.

Nor is behaviorism a reversion to stream-of-consciousness psychology.

The bottom of all these problems of body and mind, of the physical and psychological, is some need of control or of an order, be it only an order of appearances. After the long discussion of many centuries, we may now say that order and control are not "content of consciousness," not "data," not "accident," not stumbled upon as one item among others. It is a curious feature of behaviorism that its advocates have not abdicated from control either in what they say or in a passive resignation to what they find. They say that they are scientists and in spite of the silly idolatry of data-worship, the scientist is not palming off on us the uncritical appearances of his stream of consciousness. He wants evidences, tests, demonstration. Data-worship has analogy in the worship of gold as a monetary base, an assumed value divorced from all functioning in the market place of goods and services. The scientist is not rendered helpless by data. The reason is that scientific data *occur only in a controlled inquiry*. Behaviorism stems from the laboratory, not from the casual observations of a tourist. Not only so, the behaviorist proposes to become a social manager. We are to stop drifting about in unregulated ways, deluding ourselves with a "freedom" that leads us into every sort of social mess. Control reappears. It is essential to the procedure of science, and it is also essential to the application of scientific truth.

Contrast this with the status of control in nature or in the stream of consciousness. There is nothing to do about a natural regularity. It is "there," as we say. There is nothing to do about the stream of consciousness. We can have no quarrel with it. We are then faced with the rather astonishing proposal that by becoming behaviorists we can *restore control*. It purports to be a science of control, not a science of phenomena. Unlike the physicists of the seventeenth century, the behaviorist is not saying that the phenomena of nature are not what we had supposed. The earth does move, but we have no more to do with a system of gravity than with a divine arrangement. Hear Addison:

In Reason's ear they all rejoice
And utter forth a glorious voice;
For ever singing as they shine,
'The Hand that made us is divine.'

Indeed, science itself has rejoiced in showing forth a world beyond our tamperings. The word "subjective" took on the force of disqualification. To be sure, this absolute objectivity has not been persuasive. Science is discovering that it has a history and so comes under a control not operative in any laboratory. Dated time is not clock time. But the popular and even the learned view of scientific nature was, and largely remains, that of an absolute object. We keep out. We had better if we want the truth. "The trail of the serpent" is not to be over it all.

Now, it is curious that the behaviorist is proposing something quite different, although draped in the cloak of science. He is a manager, quite unlike Galileo or Newton, Boyle or Lavoisier. This requires to be accounted for. In the temper of traditional science, management is an outrage. It is precisely what one avoids as one would the plague. Science has exorcised doing and managing. It is a heresy. It is the basic heresy. Science has been viewed as having nothing to do with any doing whatsoever. It has even been disturbed by considerations suggesting that the scientist himself is in the picture, that the observer qualifies or changes what is observed. That was precisely what earlier science hoped to avoid. Keep out. We have been arrested by threat of an old subjectivism.

What is it, then, that marks off behavioral science? It is the assumption of *particular* controls of changes. We are presented not with the majestic order of change as in physics but with particular and local changes. The operative terms are "stimulus" and "response," terms wholly alien to physics and chemistry and, in fact, destructive of the whole order that they have so magnificently described. So one is faced with the perhaps astonishing fact that in nature there are no stimuli and no responses. Anyone who wants those terms is no longer dealing in natural science. Let him try them on the physicist or chemist.

And yet, as remarked above, every parent and teacher does apply stimuli and expect responses. This is the basis of the appeal of behaviorism, which in terms of natural science, is a destructive nonsense.

What then are these intruders, the "stimulus" and the "response"? In all cases they are the production of the behavioral scientist. In no case are they the objects of nature understood as parts of an unbroken order and producing other events in that same order. Behaviorism is an interruption of nature or else it is a fraud. This needs consideration because it is not unusual to hear that an alleged interruption of nature is indeed a folly and a stupidity carrying us back to chaos or else to a primitive animism.

Every stimulus is *factitious,* to use an old and Cartesian word. No stimulus is a natural object or process, like heat under a pot of water or water itself as a chemical substance.

The control of behavior presumes control in the stimulus itself. It is a controlled object, not a natural object. Pavlov had a bell. He rang it. He rang it fifty times. His control over the response reverted to his control over the stimulus. *There is no uncontrolled stimulus.* The status of a stimulus is that of an object already identified in a purposive context and in a scientific context. A bell is *not* a light. Pavlov's control assumed such distinctions, all of them resultants of functioning. How many times does one ring the bell? Neither fifty nor any other quantity is an object in nature, not zero or infinity or minus two. Nor are there clocks, yardsticks, balances in nature. None of them is a natural object. But they are the actualities of control. None of them is a "perceived" object on psychological terms.

What price, the stimulus? It is a word that has caused small dubiety or none at all. It appears without apology in Psychology 1–2. There must be some rather unforced hospitality in its general reception as an inoffensive word. But it is a loaded word. It is loaded with the controls that identify those curious objects not in nature but in function. The stimulus to behavior is an organized object, such as the bell or the once-famous colored ball enticing the infant. We do not have "child-centered education." We center it on the colored ball, which is a factitious object and *only for that reason* educative. In fact there are strenuous objections to an educational practice that treats the child as a prior reality having nothing to do with colored balls, with other factitious objects, or sometimes with quite formal objects such as numbers, yardsticks, and words. Nature is no educator.

If you want a "response," you must produce a "stimulus"; and to do so you must have intervened as the very meaning and presence of the stimulus. Any stimulus is an *actuality*. It is neither a "reality" nor an "appearance." It is a presence only because it is factitious. In nature there are no stimuli to specific responses, because nothing in nature is present and so capable of establishing a present response. There, any appearance dissolves into an order that is universal, a consideration that underlies the despair and the anxiety of the existentialist who storms about in desperation and looks on the happy pleasures of the Deer Park with alarm or with disdain. The same importance appears in James Thomson's "City of Dreadful Night." The men and women of the Romantic period embraced nature, but it was not the nature of physics. Wordsworth spoke of

> . . . a sense sublime
> Of something far more deeply interfused. . . .
> A motion and a spirit, that impels
> All thinking things. . . .

But the romantic, like the pessimist, had no constitutional place for the actual and, in the more extreme cases, abandoned the articulate world of specific controls. "We look before and after and pine for what is not."

To save behavior, along with stimulus and response, we must make them constitutional. If they are not constitutional, they fade away into physics, the stream of consciousness, or, perhaps, the supernatural in one form or another. In no such case does one keep the state of affairs that not only permits behavior but *enforces* it.

The fact is that behavior has no place in most views of the world, no essential place. For Aristotle the practical sciences were not nature defining. Emerson wrote, "Philosophically considered, the Universe is composed of Nature and the Soul," expressing the most generally held view. It is remarkable how steadily great distinctions have been made and no account given of the process of their derivation. The great distinctions have had no presentation. Such has been the lack in the great "categories" from the earliest time to Kant. We have had Space, but no yardstick; Time, but no clock; Cause, but no purposes that produce or prevent. In consequence the famous "forms" have been as persistent as they have remained mysterious, the occasion of assault or of a feeble contempt. The actual has been overlooked. And so the great Kant, as late as 1781, gave no constitutional place to yardsticks and clocks as the functioning objects, the actualities that are the source of spatial and temporal order. Einstein considered how one could allege that two clocks, in two places, could be declared synchronous, a problem at the root of Euclidean and non-Euclidean space.

All universals, all categories, are functional. They are not intellectual, not ideas within a mysterious mind, but overt and actual. It is the actual that generates all distinctions such as the finite and infinite. Finitude has been no less mysterious than infinity. Neither is content of consciousness. Neither is a perceived object.

The stimulus is always an actuality. This has been the blind spot of psychology, which has never accounted for any but a physical change as the consequence of a physical stimulus. The door was open to the behaviorist, whose stimulus, not being itself actual, produces no act, not even a reaction on the purified basis of a radical atomization, which professes to tell "how" but never "why." The term "reaction" is parasitic upon assumptions of functional order that are neither psychological nor physical.

Consider the term "stimulus." If one says "consider the 'mind' or the 'soul' or the 'universe,' " one is met with the disdain of the intellectual and even of the psychologist, whose designation would seem to imply such terms as quite proper. But on the premises of radical empiricism what in the world is a stimulus? Where is one to look? In the heavens or in Afghanistan? Is one looking for something red, green, hot, cold, of a specific gravity, size, or velocity? If you want a thoroughly mysterious word of the sort abominated by empiricists, try "stimulus." It becomes quickly evident that a stimulus has no analogy with a common noun. Not long ago there was a crying up of "ostensive definition," a remarkably foolish idea. On its presumably sensible assumptions, try pointing to something in particular that is a "stimulus" but not a violet by a mossy stone. This is a stupendous, a stupifying nonsense. Stimulus is no common noun. It is a universal. It is a wholly formal term. It is a functional term quite as much as clock, zero, an uttered word, or the definite article. The title of a famous book of William James was *A Pluralistic Universe.* Obviously, James could not use the definite article without abandoning his case, and on his premises that part of speech has no meaning. But I like novels by Fielding and Trollope because they have no villains and no saints, and so I have no intention of excommunicating James, who, viewed historically, was a great man.

The elusiveness of the term "stimulus" should put one on guard. It goes unaccounted for in any book on psychology, quite in the same way as the clock with which "reaction time" is measured.

The basic stimuli are functional objects, as when a child learns to tell time by the clock or to discriminate shapes and sizes, to put a predicate to a spoken noun. These stimuli lead to science and to universals because they are themselves actualities and not objects analogous to sticks and stones. There is no chemistry of yardsticks, for they are not specific objects and can be made of maple or steel or what you will, not what you choose, but what you will and declare. "The readiness is all." Choices fall within prior controls; will actualizes the controls. Today there is a flight from the actual, a repudiation of authority in others because there is none in oneself. The actual is both the critical and the adventurous. To say that parallel lines never meet is not to state any fact under the broad blue canopy of heaven; it is to declare a controlling presence and a historical risk. It is the actual—not the real, not the apparent, for they are derivative of act. It is not the case that the "real" order of space is non-Euclidean; it is the actual order that is so. Mathematicians have wondered whether or not they dealt in realities; they do not. They deal in actualities and *therefore* in universals and in order. The powerful and historical stimuli are such constitutional actualities.

But the stimulus is not confined to clocks, yardsticks, numbers, words, and other utterances. Anything can operate as a stimulus, and anything named has in fact so operated. It is precisely this lack of specific embodiment that sets the problem. For then we must either give up dealing in stimuli or else see them as formal, universal, and actual. The stimulus is invested with a place in a prior control. The stimuli of the advertiser—a new fashion, a tool, a cut of beef, organic vegetables—have all a factitious status. That is why they come to the notice of psychologists. They have a "meaning," as we say. This meaning is not in the occult mind of the person responding but in the occasion itself. Nothing has meaning to me that has none in itself. A meaningless world is one not presented as an actuality but as an overpowering reality, where that alleged reality fades away into the chaos of the stream of consciousness, or not even to so articulated an event, itself unknown except in utterance and presence.

It is essential, on the premises of a behaviorism that allows no prior meaning to a stimulus, to recognize that no "response" occurs. A burning glass can set leaves afire in the assumed order of nature, but it is no stimulus. Nor is it a stimulus when its focused heat is applied to that object called a nerve. Treat the nerve, or the whole "nervous system"—a vague term—as an object, and very soon the problem of what then happens gets taken over by the physicists and chemists, for whom there is no difference between the nervous system and the solar system in the mode of describing its phenomena or order. *But for them there is no "behavior."*

None of the "units of account" in physics and chemistry is an object. They keep accounts in terms of numbers and of numerically expressed modes of events, such as centimeters, grams, seconds, or volts. No object is mentioned and certainly no pigeon. All such units of account are functioning objects, and they are enormously stimulating, indeed, infinitely so, so that we now have a very sub-atom called a "quark." Of course, that is to say in the *course* set by purely functional objects, one word leads to another. If a man wants the "terminal" satisfaction of John Dewey he should avoid words, for he won't find them there. But it is precisely these infinities that occur as the actual present and nowhere else. There is joy in parents, perhaps in heaven, when a child can count to three. Of *course* he will have to go further, into very puzzling consequences. There is a terminal satisfaction no more in "three" than in the notorious and disreputable thirty.

In all this I have been trying to say a good word for behavior, for stimulus and response. The easy popularity of those words suggest familiarity and acceptance. We do not, as a rule, feel hostile to stimulating occasions and may seek them out, pay money for them. Nor do we usually feel helpless or put upon in this recognition of objects already invested with meaning, embodying action, purpose, or will. Every word in the dictionary has that force, every work of art, every historical act, every equation of physical science. If nature abhors a vacuum, so does a response. Every response presumes a prior response, however vague. A stimulus is a force, as any word is also a command and a responsibility. And one may note that there is no proposal of "stimulus-responsibility." The reason is not that there is a stimulus but no responsibility but that there is *no stimulus* that is not *already* an embodiment of control. So, it is not surprising to find a proposal that men require control so that their uncontrolled responses will at least avoid disaster, or what someone so regards. Control driven out of the front door creeps back through the window, or perhaps the skylight. So I have not been dismissing behavior but proposing to make it constitutional, an element of structure, not an episode in an alien world or in a chaos.

Mathematics and physics are the best policed sciences

because their units of account are explicit and wholly functional. They are entirely secular. It is our story. But those sciences have at least had the grace to raise questions about their units of account. So has logic. There are other areas of inquiry, including psychology and what is called "political science," where units of account hardly occur. There are "schools" of psychology. But it is certain that any unit of account is a functioning object, not a perceived object.

It rates a word to note that one's yardstick, while neither an appearance nor a reality, entails the psychological in the qualities of vision and touch. So does all utterance. It is apropos of the functioning object that we are at pains to sharpen sensation and not let it drift. Sensation has a role to play, but no role until it serves in the more precise observation of functioning actualities. The rest is drift, but a drift for which, on the premises, there is not even a name. It is fair to ask what it could have been that brought sensation to notice as a psychological factor. What excuse is offered for so much as identifying it? I have never found one in a book on psychology. Sensation is a structure word. It does not occur within the limits of the psychological but is rather one of the units of account that define the psychological component of experience.

My problem was "What price, behavior?" I have suggested how to give it status and authority. We do indeed need to control it. The control lies in identifying the stimulus. The stimulus to a response is an actuality. The control is there, and it is inherent in the stimulus itself, in a yardstick, clock, word, or even the dinner bell.

9

The Stimulus as Local Control

The more I look at the claims of behaviorism, the more I feel that its appeal derived in part, in large part, from the neglect of local efficacy in both science and philosophy. It was not only science that disparaged local control but philosophy as well. The scientist may reject Aristotle's final cause, but the control of events in Aristotle was not local. It was a total order. Changes in the particular had an order in a general setting. But the local was not the controller of changes. In this respect the philosopher has not differed from the scientist. The dispute was over the account given of the total control. It was not over a rivalry of the total and the local.

All the early philosophers moved away from magic and from a primitive animism. They were animists in their view of the cosmos, not in acceptance of efficacy in particular or individual souls.

Science did not differ with philosophy in that conviction that the whole was to account for the particular. It gave a different story of the whole. The exorcism of purpose-control from particulars was common to both. Philosophy preserved a psychic control in the totality; science kept the totality but got rid of its psychic quality. Neither had a constitutional place for the particular, for the individual, for local control, for the here-and-now, for the actual.

The behaviorist now proposes to restore the control of particulars. At least some events are not to be referred to a totality, either psychic or nonpsychic.

This leaves the behaviorist in an uncomfortable position. As a scientist he refers all changes to regularity of a universal sort. Yet his own science, or alleged science, describes particular changes as consequences of particular controls. The thrust of natural science has been toward a uniform and universal order; the behavioral scientist claims to see particular determinants of events. The result is as much an attack on natural science and its nonpsychic totality as upon certain philosophers who have urged a psychic totality. Behaviorism wants a local control that is neither scientific nor philosophical, in so far as philosophy has proposed a totality, but a psychic one.

The operative idea is the "stimulus." This is the source of local change. It is neither physically nor psychically defined. It appeals to no sort of total order as the explanation of its efficacy.

The result is that the "stimulus" is closer to an antique magic than to either the physical or the psychic view of a general control of changes.

In view of the prestige of scientific uniformities and of the proclaimed scientific status of behaviorism, it is arresting to note the reception it has received from people who profess allegiance to a scientific world.

It is arresting until one notes that the scientific temper has not uncommonly been associated with a claim to local control.

On the other side, scientific knowledge has also been a strong influence in reducing supposed power to impotence.

Behaviorism is a revolt from scientific impotence, an essay in the restoration of local control, but without psychic control.

Those who have felt a propriety in a psychic view of totality face an analogous problem in behaviorism. They have attempted to keep a local control in action, or in the rational mind, or both. But they do not relish the behav-

iorist view of such local control. They want a place for the
"stimulus" and for the "response." In that they join the
behaviorist, as the physical scientist does not do. And so it
is toward those who accept local control, but on psychic
grounds, that behaviorism directs its attack. It is these who
cannot ignore the behaviorist, because they accept his basic
claim, and now, consequently, offer the major objections.

The curious feature of these controversies occurs in the
dubious status of any but a universal control, both for the
scientist and the psychist. "Knowledge is power," but
"nature to be commanded must be obeyed," where even
obedience carries the flavor of disobedience, or of non-
obedience, as a possibility to be avoided, an absurdity on
premises of universal control. On the side of the psychist
there has been the long and notorious controversy over
free will. This debate was not staged with a scientific
antagonist. It was a domestic quarrel within the limits of
psychism. A totalitarian and psychic explanation of events
allowed no constitutional status to local control. In this
respect scientism and psychism are the same.

Along comes the behaviorist. He says he is a scientist—
but he exercises a local control. He says he is no psychist,
but, like the psychist, he wants local control. What is he?
A magician? In so far as he, or anybody, does not attribute
events to a universal control, scientific or psychic, what
else could he be if not a magician? For the sake of local
control Faust sold his soul to the devil, who could perform
all sorts of magic tricks, including power over the behavior
of others. Glendower could call spirits from the vasty deep.
The point is not in the peculiar method used; it is in any
claim whatsoever to a control that is local and not universal.

To get a local event that is not to be lost in the universal,
scientific or psychic, one has to employ a local cause or
control. This is the "stimulus." It is a local power or force.
It produces the equally local "response." But neither the
scientific nor the psychic totality can tolerate a local power
to produce a local change.

One would expect the learned to regard the behaviorist

as an utterly mindless man, a primitive, a throw-back, a wizard, a fraud. Not at all; they show a sharp interest. They are wary and reserved but quite openly attracted, as if there might be something in it. The fear expressed that the behavioral engineer will rob us of our "freedom" is only half-hearted. What learned man—scientist or psychist— avows a world that permits any autonomy? For all that, there is also only a half-hearted avowal of some order that prevents autonomy. The pluralism of James has won considerable acceptance as a way out of the "block universe." The "indeterminacy" of Heisenberg receives a recurrent notice, as if, like pluralism, it offered relief from some ordered totality.

(One may note, in passing, that the nonempirical status of "cause," and so its reduction to a "pseudo-concept," has not alerted these amateurs to the realization that irregularity is no more empirical than is causal restraint.)

It seems that nearly everyone cherishes the idea of a local control and welcomes attempts to make it plausible. Still, it goes against the grain if one is a scientist or a psychist to admit or claim an interruption of the order that, supposedly, makes the world intelligible.

On the whole the emphasis of the learned has been on some order that absorbs all local events. Order is heaven's first law; every event has a cause; not a sparrow falleth; the real is the rational. There is extensive testimony to a strong preoccupation with the idea of a prevailing order.

On the other hand, the evidence of order has had to make an appearance. This appearance is control of particulars. Put it in reverse: where there is no particular and local control, no general order can so much as be suggested. An empiricism that has found no local control—no act—has also been unable to find any general order. Our natural scientists are uncomfortable with local controls; consequently they are also suspicious of a general order, and they say that they can tell no more than "how" events occur, never "why" they occur. The reason is that the word "why" presumes a universal, and no universal falls within the empirical. But there is another factor in this suspicion of local control; it suggests a controller and so an agent, a force of some sort that accounts for particular events. Science never accounts for a particular event, because to do so it would require a particular control. So it forsakes both a general and a local control. It avoids any sort of control. It is not usually noted that the current reason for the aversion of science to local control is not that local control interrupts a general order, but rather that not even a general order can be empirically found. There is no general order to be interrupted. I remember a good lecture by a scientist in which he scoffed at what he called the *"a priori."* He found nothing of that sort. In consequence he had neither a local nor a general control. He had phenomena, or so claimed, conjunctions, but no enforcements either general or specific.

The conclusion: where there is no local control neither is there a general order. The manifestation and evidence of a general order requires a local control. Without local control no general order can put in an appearance. Where order does not put in an appearance, it cannot be suggested, much less affirmed.

The consequence has been that local control has always seemed a miracle or something like a miracle, a wonder, an arrest, a revelation. But it should be noted that the objection to miracle is not necessarily based on a premise of a general order that a miracle interrupts. It is based on a denial of a general order, which could then be interrupted. When people believed that they had experienced a miracle it was because they had never doubted that a general control could be made manifest. Moses could perform all sorts of credible miracles, but Jesus could not. The universal control was not made manifest in Jesus, but this did not lead His contemporaries to repudiate the miraculous. Far from it. To this day Judaism celebrates the general order that was made manifest by Moses and Aaron. Jehovah is not Aristotle's prime mover, the inherent final cause of all changes.

It needs notice that the miracle was regarded not as an interruption of a general order but as its manifestation in appearance. The current view is that no appearance manifests an order, whether general or local. Allege any order in appearance and you are put down as an apriorist, dogmatist, a victim of superstition. It is true that the prescientific mind did find revelations of order in appearance. That no such revelation occurs is the current claim of the scientific temper. This is the basis of our current anarchy.

It is not just a matter of recognizing that a conviction of local control dies hard. It is rather that no control whatever is now credited. The disparagement of local control seems to many to result from a belief in a general control. But we are neither stoics nor epicureans. Even the "world I never made" is out of fashion and so all the crying and bewailing to which it gave rise. Nor, with Margaret Fuller, do we "accept the universe."

So, the problem of local control is more serious than is supposed by those who cling to a belief in general order. The disclosure is now that, lacking any local control, we have no evidence of a general order. The local efficacy that would proclaim the general order, and would stand as its evidence and warrant, is not permitted. And so there is no general order. We are nihilists. Our dissenters characteristically attack the embodiments of local order—the police, firemen, courts, Congress, the flag, academic requirements, grades, elitism, hierarchy of any sort. No one is to fail. No one commits a crime. There is no treason. It is hard to say whether the "media" deal in unengaged gossip or whether they are panders to accidental interests. I mention these phenomena in order to avoid the charge that the problem of local control is an empty technicality in a useless discourse.

But once again we are meeting a claim of local control. That is behaviorism. But something new has been added. It is that such control is not an intrusion but a necessity. Without such control we are adrift. The early scientists sought out the order of nature. Their aim was to discover what was not under local control. They were not interfering or pretending to be in charge. On the whole, the nature so discovered was humiliating. What we did seemed a trifle. "Why so hot, little man?" But now one hears that such knowledge is not enough. Nobel prizewinners in natural science yearn to become "activists." They tell us what to do, or what we ought to do. I know a scientist who told me with great sobriety or solemnity that we needed to study "values." The universe was in no trouble. It went its usual calm way. But we were in trouble and something should be done about it. We needed a local control. If there were any "values," they would have to be found in (or applied to) the here-and-now, not in nature. Nothing was amiss there, nor anything right, either, of course. The times, however, were out of joint, not a recent discovery.

Behaviorism is the acknowledgment that without local control we are adrift. That is its startling disclosure. This claim is made by persons who regard themselves as scientists. From the temple of science now emanates the oracular announcement that we can no longer let nature take its course. One would expect that the objection to behaviorism would be most vocal from scientific quarters. If scientists had a proper sense of their own historic victory, their immense achievement as the revealers of nature, they would now protest this reversion to particular influences, to changes attributed to something called a "stimulus." Instead, one finds that objection to behaviorism is most vocal from those who had never abandoned the belief in local control, imagining that they freely went to the post office and respected their neighbors as also capable of autonomy and responsibility, of self-control and self-correction. These are the people who resist behaviorism. But the basis of their objection is not an aversion to local control. They are, rather, firm believers in their ability to be guided by circumstances. They respond to a word spoken, to an idea, to the dinner bell, and even to the behaviorist himself. But—and this is the breaking point—they claim to exercise some discretion in such responses to circumstance. In so far as the behaviorist emphasizes the operative effect of a particular circumstance they have no quarrel with him. But they differ over the account given of that occasion and of the response to it. That is the locus of their dispute. They are, then, more closely allied with the behavioral account of action than with any totalitarian control.

A key factor in this dispute is the account given of the "stimulus." Neither party denies its efficacy. But this efficacy will depend on what one takes the stimulus to be.

One might, then, pose the question "What is the 'nature' of the stimulus?" That question is loaded. For the stimulus is no part of nature. As the price of not relapsing into totalitarian explanations, physical or psychic, the behaviorist has to avoid treating the stimulus as part of nature. No local response can endure a totalitarian explanation. It must have a local explanation, if any.

One has to consider the possibility that the behaviorist is prepared to settle for the absolute coincidence of "stimulus" and "response" where no connection is claimed. It becomes, then, a "concomitant variation," as with J. S. Mill. If one does so, one must then settle for the sacrifice of control. That is not the way the behaviorist presents his case. He is not telling us about the events in his private stream of consciousness. In fact, he is not dealing in consciousness at all and prefers to avoid that non-empirical idea. Response is not to be accounted for in terms of the effect of a stimulus on consciousness. Such a story smacks of a control other than that of the stimulus and suggests an independence that is at the root of our illusions of freedom. The laboratory object, the supposed animal that responds to the stimulus, is not regarded as nothing more than another item in a stream of consciousness, and neither is the stimulus. So I lay aside the abstract possibility that the behaviorist is operating with absolute concomitant variations in a passive stream of consciousness where nothing is under control. This should help to locate the problem.

The particularity of the stimulus as an efficacy is the crux. We have to recognize, however, that the particular has never had the attention or the status of the universal. Behaviorism is now forcing attention on the particular as a control.

That is where it has to be met if at all.

What, then, endows the particular with efficacy? It is the

process that has made it particular. For the particular is not a datum; it is a status in an organization. But such an organization is not that of the totalitarian, where no particular appears. It is the organization of the individual as functioning. The particular is a "meaning" generated in functioning. The term "meaning" has been elusive on psychological premises, that is, on premises of passivity. On such premises there is no efficacy. The limiting control of a stimulus is the consequence of the actual functioning that has already operated to select and characterize any stimulus that has the power to specify a response. The effective stimulus—particular, limited, and limiting—has already been touched by the local, which is functioning. The dinner bell is a meaning because there *has been* eating. It is not the case that such a stimulus is a wholly accidental "association." It is notorious that passive association entails no "response."

Some force *other* than the alleged associated phenomena has, in fact, had to be invoked to account for anything *done* about them. Mill, for example, blandly invokes "utility"—a rabbit out of a hat if there ever was one. The behaviorist wants a *continuity* between stimulus and response—a very sensible idea. Whether or not he gets it will depend on the account he gives of the stimulus. That is his vulnerable point. On his terms he cannot say why in the world there should be a stimulus—a specific efficacy to a specific event. Specific efficacy is scientific nonsense. Nor is it what the behaviorist settles for. Like Mill, he then has to propose to take charge of these nonrational conjunctions and become a social engineer.

But while I hold these considerations to be valid, I believe, too, that some larger warrant is required, some *affirmative* order that gives them force. My affirmation is the midworld. The stimulus has force because it is *not* an object but a *functioning object*. That is its status. It has been specified in functioning. The particular is a *consequence* of functioning and is original and constitutional. It is not psychological. It is not physical. It is actual. That is why the act, which is always limited, answers to the limited stimulus.

The behaviorist is right in objecting to the stimulus as a "perception." He is not joining those who see action—or what has been so called—as a superimposed consequence of an alleged perception with which the perceiver had nothing to do and then, subsequently, in a mysterious way, is to do something about. He wants continuity. So do I.

In this way behaviorism is a historically important development. In its basic interest it is not a mistake. It is the interest in the particular as efficacious. To take a broad contrast, consider the long influence of Boethius, widely read and translated. The *Consolation* is an evidence of the disparagement of the particular and actual. Its sources are classical and Christian. The emphasis is on a reconciling totality. It is a noble and eloquent work, not less so because also popular. But it affirms a world in which the actual has no constitutional place. The particular is not controlling. It is not controlling because it is not defined. It is elusive and fades away into a totality.

Behaviorism focuses on the particular event. It is not totalitarian. It asserts a local control. But the alleged control has no constitutional force. The particular is not *itself* the actuality of control. That is why the behaviorist needs to become a social engineer. The freedom that he disparages is in the particular itself as a factor in the organization of the actual. The functioning that identifies particulars is itself freedom. It is the source of all distinctions.

What I affirm is the metaphysical status of the particular. It is purely organizational term. It is a universal. It is not a common noun. It is particular because standing as a "meaning," not as an abrupt and magical datum to which action is incidental, subsequent, and arbitrarily engineered. None of the powerful stimuli is a datum, an arbitrary object—not the yardstick, clock, balance, word, monument. They stand in functioning and are original and free. They are the midworld, neither appearance nor reality, but actuality. They are the controllers of appearances and separate error and illusion from the real. Control appears in the actual. It is notorious that it has failed to *appear* anywhere else—in psychology, physics, or theology.

I call myself a free man because my stimuli are factors of a functioning immediacy. Order is the form of functioning, of present active participles.

By all means let us have an efficacious stimulus, and so a continuity of stimulus and response. If we have that, we can dispense with the social engineer, a desperate fellow who wants to take charge of a world not defined and revealed in his own functioning actuality. Those who see you as put upon need not, of course, have any qualms about taking charge of you.

10

Conditioning Is Particular

Physics is a model for behaviorism in so far as no value control is to operate in behavioral science. Does this mean that the behaviorist is a physicist or a chemist? Physics does more than exorcise value-control. It has *other controls*—centimeters, grams, seconds, volts, quantity. In those terms it gives us equations where no specific object or event is named. Its results are uniformities. This is nature as order. Nothing there is "conditioned." Nature is unconditioned. Experiment reproduces or discovers an order that we can *not* modify. Dropping weights at Pisa, or here at the physics lab, does nothing to change nature's ways. It is those *unchanging* ways that science explores.

This is not what the behaviorist discloses. His studies have not revised the *laws* of nature. He has not split the atom or discovered a new "element" or rectified atomic weights. Nor, in more particular ways, does he invent plastics or a new blast furnace in a steel mill. So, although he is like a physicist in getting rid of value-control, he adds nothing to the story told by physics or any natural science. This, I think, may well give one pause. The claim of affinity with natural science bears no fruit, has had no consequences, either in the *general* laws of nature or in the *particular* and technical application of those regulations to special purposes.

The nonpersonal story of nature told by physics did not, however, get told in the absence of value-control. The region disclosed was not governed by value, by purpose, or by will; but the *investigator* himself did not claim that his *study* had no value-control. At the least, natural science saved men from error and superstition. It was a way, a chief way, for the discovery of truth. It also was a discovery of the mind, person, ego. The discoverer found his freedom in geometry, logic, astronomy. Plato required geometry. It was the unscientific man who was confused, helpless, not aware of his power. The human being was distinctively a pursuer of knowledge, said Aristotle.

Similarly, although Archimedes told only about nature's nonpersonal ways, he could find out useful facts, such as the relation of weight to volume.

The nonpersonality of nature was not, then, taken to suggest the absence of value-control in the scientist or operator. This is in contrast with "behavioral science," which has claimed to exorcise value-control not only from nature, but from the operator as well.

Now, instead of seeing nature as evidence of our freedom and power, we are to see it as a proof of our lack of power.

This result is related to the failure of behavioral science to affect our view of nature, as mentioned above. Impotence did not discover nature; behaviorism, denying power, has no story to tell about nature. The region of nature, appealed to as *proof* of the absence of value-control is not discovered by behavioral science. It adds nothing to our knowledge of nature as described by physics. This seems to me an important, but overlooked, consideration.

The conclusion: behaviorism is *no part of natural science.* It presents no nonpersonal region where vast regularities define all change. In that nonpersonal region there is no "stimulus," no "response," no "conditioning," no intrusion of any operator in the inherent order of change.

Nature was discovered as the order that *no one can change* by his purposes. Yet this discovery did not nullify the discoverer. It gave him status. The mind was disclosed as nature was disclosed.

Behaviorism *forbids* the discovery of nature. It manipu-

lates. Nature was discovered as an order *not* to be manip-
ulated.

It is not the case that nature removes value-control. On
the contrary, it is the principal source of our *assurance* of
such control. It made control possible. Natural science was
not a consequence of pure thought. It developed from the
acts and purposes of men. It assisted action, even in geometry, as in measuring land or calculating the location of a
ship approaching a harbor. The universal was of enormous
assistance to action. Why? Because it made clear the *form*
of the act. It separated the controlling form from the circumstances, so that one could count goats as well as sheep.
It was the counting that was the doing. One was not
"responding" to sheep or goats or camels but acting in a
wholly general way. The behaviorist "response" does not
account for any universal. That is why it does not account
for nature, the nature to which it appeals for the impersonal. That, also, is why it can present no action. Action,
one's own deed, grew out of universals. When men learned
something about the order of counting, measuring, speaking, reasoning, then for the first time they could act. A
man could say, "I made a mistake." He did it. I did it. You
did *not* do it.

This quite nonscientific status of behaviorism leaves it
more akin to an episodic animism than to the order of
nature. It attempts to control events where no universal
control is admitted, where none can be discovered, where
the actual state of affairs that led to the search for universals
is not recognized. The whole story of natural science as an
achievement, a triumph of power, a victory over a wander-
ing helplessness, cannot be told on behaviorist terms.
Behaviorism cannot allow power.

Science did not exorcise animism. It exorcised purpose-
control from *nature,* but it could do so only because it did
not exorcise control from the scientist and from his self-
controlled functioning.

Behaviorism denies self-control *because* it allows no natural science.

In terms of nature the operations of the behaviorist are a

hocus-pocus magic. Nothing in nature submits to the operations of the behaviorist. The behaviorist generates no universal. That is because he does not act. The universal is the form of act. It is notorious that in the absence of act, in the passivity of reception of "data," no universal is found. In terms of impotence and passivity all universals are "pseudo-concepts."

The behaviorist has no causal order. Cause is undiscoverable apart from action, the act that produces or *prevents* an event. Cause is a control word. Nature appears only in consequence of such controls—of mathematics, of logic, and of dialectic, that is, of self-control.

None of the "units of account" in which nature is defined is an object. All are functional and organizational, including the atom, as well as the inch, or second, or zero. None is an object of perception. All disclose the midworld.

Behaviorism has no unit of account in which nature is defined. All units of account are acts, pure acts. They are actual, not "real" not "apparent," neither objects within nature nor in the stream of consciousness. They are the incarnate word. Without that there is no presence.★

I can bring water to boil. How does that differ from my bringing a supposed person to stop at a red light? It differs in that water is *identified* by temperatures and pressures. It solidifies at 32°F, vaporizes at 212°F. That is its "nature." I cannot change it. If a liquid does *not* freeze at 32°F, then it is not water, alcohol perhaps. But you ask for water, alcohol, or some chemical for your car radiator. You do not ask for water that has been "conditioned" not to freeze at 32°F. Water is water is water, a profound discovery of Gertrude Stein to which she owes her literary reputation.

★One could—one has to—consider why Christianity took such hold. It was the incarnate word. It was the presence. It gave a center in a dissolute world, morally and intellectually dissolute. But that is another and fascinating story. Still, one may note that it was the Greek attempt to establish the controlling *present* that was appropriated by Christianity—a troubled alliance. But it seems hardly sensible to turn away from such powerful influences.

If one can answer the question "What is it?" then one is stating a "nature," naming a thing, object, or substance. In so far as "it" has a name, it is not something conditioned. If you buy alcohol for your radiator, you are not paying money to buy something unknown and nameless on the assurance that something or other has been conditioned not to burst your radiator below 32°F.

Now for the traffic light. Something or other vaguely referred to as "you" stops at the light. On the analogy of water or any other substance one would then have to say that you are *identified* as stopping at lights. That is your definition and constitution. If you did not stop, you would not be you but Miller. That's Miller to the core, a non-stopper. Just as it is better to use alcohol in cold weather so it is better to ride with you and to avoid Miller, a non-stopper.

But the behavioristic psychologist does not equate you and Miller with such changes. He says that to stop or not to stop is a phenomenon produced by "conditioning." This *dissociates* some things vaguely called you and Miller from the phenomenon of stopping. There is no connection between *them* and whatever brings about stopping, quite unlike the state of affairs when water, a liquid of molecular composition, takes to boiling or freezing in relation to heat, an energy that is part of its own constitution in all its states.

I may feel a momentary gratification in not being regarded as a congenital non-stopper, just as the behaviorist says. It may come as a relief. I am not necessarily a non-stopper. I am assured of that by the behaviorist. Many people seem to find such assurances agreeable. Oh, yes, they stop, or do not, speak a language, go to church, play tennis, associate with Mary or John—but in no case is that what they *are*. All such changes are "behavior." All have been "conditioned." I am no more an English speaker or a lover of Mary than I am a non-stopper.

The conditioned object is never what it seems. Water is precisely what it seems. It is not conditioned. Appearance and reality meet in that substance, and in all others.

But in so far as I am *not* an English speaker, a non-stopper at lights, a tennis or soccer player, I am not what I seem. In so far as all change in me is seen as "response" to stimuli, the subject of the sentence "I am a non-stopper at red traffic lights" has no definition.

The denial of freedom or autonomy to persons, a denial made by behaviorists, is not, therefore, surprising. They are not saying "There you are and you are not free, not self-controlled." On behaviorist premises they can give no definition to the *subject* of the sentence. The predicate "non-stopper at red traffic lights" lacks a subject. Consequently, the same people who are ready to find some merit in behavior as influenced by conditioning draw back at the complete nullification of any person who is to be viewed as conditioned in *all* that he does.

The statement "All my behavior is conditioned" can be neither proved nor disproved as true or false about any *subject* of discourse.

I believe it would be in point to associate the influence of behavioral nullification with the current temper that shrinks from personal identification with all activities. No one is to be identified with the system, with a college, nation, language, historical outlook, or with the rules of traffic control. Behaviorism, appearing as a doctrine of control, becomes a doctrine of anarchy. Where all behavior is conditioned, all behavior becomes accidental and lawless. No law controls conditioning. We are what we happen to be. This is quite different from the older view of a universal sway of a regular nature of which one is part. There, all is as it must be inexorably. There, nothing is conditioned.

Behaviorism is *the repudiation of nature* and its laws. This is the true force of its accidental view of events. Behaviorism, which appears as an attack on "freedom," is an attack on nature and on science. The antagonist of freedom used to be *necessity;* it has now become the anarchic.

Nature appeared as a dispelling of anarchy, of confusion and drift. It appeared as the necessary, as law and order, as mathematical, logical, dialectical. Freedom had to struggle against necessity. But freedom has now to struggle against anarchy. That is its other and original frustration.

It is idle to attempt to put behaviorism in any "frame of reference." It has no environment. It is neither an order nor the consequence of order. That is why one cannot argue with a behaviorist. Argument assumes the unconditioned as its force and authority. It is precisely the unconditioned that behaviorism does not find.

The fact is that some people do stop at traffic lights. They have learned to do so. We have had to learn *all* particular responses—or acts—from particular occasions. That there are what are "stimuli," controls of "response" or, if not controls, at least occasions, is all that the behaviorist can propose.

The term "stimulus" is a purely formal word. On the procedures of the empiricists—Locke, Berkeley, Hume—nothing appears as a stimulus. It is a mysterious word. One cannot produce a "stimulus" as an object of perception, any more than one can produce a cause. It is not animal, vegetable, or mineral. It is an organization word.

The characteristic of a "stimulus-reponse" relation occurs as an explanation of a *particular* event, like stopping at a light. Natural science observes particulars, but its explanations pass into a general order. An eclipse of the moon is taken in stride by the astronomer who sees nothing astonishing in it. He expects it, "predicts" it. The reason why natural science does not deal in purpose-control is that it does not deal in *particular* events. Purpose appears as the alleged control of particular events. Far from disqualifying a natural order, purpose-control has thrived on it. We make ice cubes in the freezer, where the temperature is below 32°F. This permits me to offer you a cocktail. Nor does science exclude the controls of ordered functioning, as in mathematical order—constitutional sorts of action, as are also telling time or making inferences. Science could not, has not, operated without those functioning objects. They are all *actualities,* not realities, not appearances.

But the factor *omitted* in scientific explanation is the event that requires a special and *particular* explanation. Natural scientists shrug this off. They tend to treat my making ice cubes and your having a cocktail as events of no importance, trivialities in the vast invariance of nature.

Still, neither in the dim past nor in our own infancies did we begin with conscious universals; no, not even with numbers and composed spaces. We began, rather, with vague perceptions and fumbling acts out of which developed both rule and purpose. It was all messy, unclear, not articulated, something like the "big, blooming, buzzing confusion" of William James. But to call it confusion is an anachronism. As a young child, I felt no confusion. It is only on a basis of order that one identifies confusion. The drawings on the caves of Neanderthal man reveal a lucidity of definition, a directness of apprehension that contrasts with the unstable confusions of Picasso. It is true that early man was animistic, but this is not to say that he entertained the idea of ghosts or spirits. His animism was *incorporate* and particular. The separate soul and the separate body were much later seen as conscious distinctions, made explicit by Plato in *Phaedo,* a work still read in order to discover what considerations seemed to enforce the difference. Objects were distinguished, a spring from a tree, and were dealt with as different, although the spring was a Naiad and the tree a Dryad. Response, behavior, action, whatever one calls it, was addressed to particulars and was itself particular. The animate was incorporate and the object animated.

These particulars gave way to universals because they carried similarities of action. Both Naiads and Neriads were *water* nymphs. Oaks and olives were both trees. Universals emerged, both class names and those other universals that are constitutional, such as number, space, change. Pure science—that is, mathematics and physics—resulted in uniformities, which appeared to leave no status to particulars and to the changes effected by particulars. The exorcism of purpose-control, that is, of control in particular changes, says no more than that in the control of action there are factors that appear in *any action,* namely number, space, time, difference, and all other "categories." But these universal factors were never, and are not today, divorced from particulars or from the action that defined and discovered particulars. Indeed, the supposed divorce of universal acts, such as counting, from particular acts, such as counting one's money, has resulted in the amazing question whether the order of quantity has illustration and application. We scorn the base degrees by which we have risen. The "pure" mathematician cannot say that he has two feet, just because one plus one make two. Perhaps the order of numbers applies to his feet, perhaps not. How he would decide becomes a rather amusing piece of nonsense, and books get written about it by men of intellectual reputation. This seems to be a disclosure of great scope. It shows how far we are from any actual view of ourselves and of nature.

Behaviorism marks an attempt to *restore* the particular object and the particular effect of such objects. It is fair to ask what could prompt such a restoration. Why are we not satisfied to get lost in nature's vast uniformities or, perhaps, in Brahma or in the haze of nothingness? Why balk?

Notice, however, that it is the behaviorist himself who balks. As an avowed scientist he hasn't a leg to stand on. He should reduce his alleged "response" to gravity and atoms and not meddle with an absurd "conditioning"— absurd in terms of natural science. He resembles an old magician rather than a physicist. He is restoring, or claiming to restore, a *local control*. On his premises this is an unabashed interruption of nature, an unwarranted intrusion.

Here one needs to be careful. One has to avoid disparaging nature by introducing an *alien* purpose-control. One has to avoid doing just what the behaviorist is doing when he intervenes, interrupts, intrudes, and nullifies the order of nature as described in physics and mathematics. If purpose-control is to be exorcised because it is *alien* to nature, then so is the control of the behaviorist. For he is alleging that there are changes to be accounted for by particulars such as bells, traffic lights, and colored balls.

I believe it would be difficult to reject the behaviorist's claim that there are events that get referred for their explanation to what is *no part of nature*. There are controls not appearing within the limits of physics. These controls govern "response," a word indicating a local change effected by particular objects or state of affairs.

If you want "response," you have to invoke an order, or a control, not found *within* nature. But there is nature, which seems to block any such particular response to a particular and *because* it is a particular. Either nature and no response, or else a non-naturally controlled event. Such is the dilemma.

I propose to escape between the horns. How so? Because nature as an articulate region is itself an extension of functioning and is not an object. Nature as universal, and particulars as locally controlling, both developed from the actual. They are resultants, not absolute "data"—that idolatrous idea, which allows neither universals nor particulars.

Functioning is not animistic. It is the basis for discovering both body and mind. Neither is it physical.

One may say, "If one cannot so much as count, measure, tell time, then one has no idea of nature." But numbers are very peculiar objects. Eyeglasses and hearing aids do not fit one to deal with zero or prime numbers. Numbers are functioning objects. They are utterances. What one controls is utterance. It is the same in logic, or even in grammar. Any revision of nature *evolves from utterance,* as in the recent case of the relation of clocks and yardsticks. Savages have adequate eyes, but they have no Einstein. It is this articulate order that has not been made by them explicit and controlling. Nature is the projection of such controls. They are the actual, the immediate, the present. They are immediate because they *mediate* between the person and the object. They are what I call the midworld.

These functioning objects—I avoid saying "functional"—are as specific as sticks and stones. You see a yardstick, you handle it, but what you do *not* do is to treat it like a piece of wood. It may not be wood. No matter (yes, no *matter!*). But it is controlling. It is a controlling object. It is a command. It is a regulator: as we say, a "ruler." One treats it with a peculiar care and respect, like a boundary marker which to move was once a crime.

Here you have "response" and a continuing response, not one of those "terminating" responses of the instrumentalists. A man who treats a yardstick, a clock, a number, a word, a work of art as an instrument is a barbarian. Nature itself looms only as the projection of a present functioning of functioning objects. The "purest" mathematician needs to utter numbers and for that he must speak with his tongue, make marks on sand or papyrus, cut notches in a stick, string beads on wires. Pure thought is pure act. It is act that responds to act, to the embodied form of action.

So I say, let us by all means join the behaviorist in his basic premise of nature's order. But there is a price. It is that nature be articulated in the act. The act does not interfere or intrude; it *generates* nature and all its revisions. You won't find any act *within* nature, as behaviorists—and plenty of others—so unquestioningly presume. So they lose nature itself, forgetting the actualities of which it is the authoritative consequence. The powerful authority of nature derives from a present doing, the locus and immediacy of a universal order. I do not wonder that Empedocles thought himself in league with divinity or that Horace would touch the stars with his exalted head.

Not all response is "pure." Not all response is to the purely actual, to numbers, yardsticks, clocks, balances. Such responses are late. They are science. We also respond to traffic lights and whistles. But what is the status of such "stimuli"? What gives them their power? I'll put the implausible and general answer first. The particular stimulus is *not a particular object in nature*. What is more—and worse to say—there are no particular objects in nature as described by physics. The particular object, acting as stimulus to response, is itself identified *as particular* only because of its dependence on action.

Notice that a stimulus is not defined by psychological qualities. It is not a stimulus because it is red, not green or yellow, a color rather than a sound. "Stimulus" is a status word or, as I usually say, an "organization word"—quite as much so as space, time, number, and so on. This status is its *particularity*. It appears and operates as "this," as "here," "now." Nothing so ordered lacks position in an act or functioning. A "this," "here," "now" is not come upon abruptly. This object occurs in a continuum. It is "this," not "that," a distinction requiring a basis for discrimination. Such a basis is no universal. Gravity, number, atoms do not define or present *this* stone, or a stone rather than another particular. Particularity is itself a formal universal. Anything is as much particular as it is spatial or temporal.

Any particular is recognized in the course of action, dry wood for a fire, a flinty stone to strike a spark. Seeing some wood, one may decide to pitch camp on a trip to Canada's wilds. Not every place along a river or lake has dry wood. I found it so. Such particular objects have to be found out in the course of experience, as we say. They are not revelations or miraculous data. Particulars are no more, or less, original than universals. Both emerge from the functioning actuality. Every particular so discriminated occupies a status in action. That is its "meaning." We "respond" to such particular meanings. When one "misbehaves" it is because one has missed the meaning of an object in another person's cause of action. The stimulus is a meaning.

Particularity is no more a *perceived* object than is any other constitutional factor of experience or of a world. It is organizational and therefore functioning. One needs to account for particularity as much as for universality.

There has long been great joy in the philosophic heaven over the discovery of universals. In the seventeenth century it was usual to speak of scientists as "philosophers," and colleges still have chairs of natural philosophy in the department of physics. But the other factor of an individual experience—the particulars, the local, the this-here-now—has been neglected. There were reasons for it. Transmissible knowledge appeared as a general order, especially as geometry. One may well say that science is what can be transmitted and taught. The local, the partic-

ular, the individual, the this-here-now of experience, its
existential factor, cannot be expressed in regularities or
uniformities. It occurs as presence. The teacher of the
humanities cannot speak for something else. The scientist
can say, does say, that he speaks for nature: the prophet for
God. But the humanities speak only *for themselves* and speak
in the immediate authority and presence of the poet, the
historical agent, or the teacher himself. I remember being
upset because it was said of my course in Plato that there
was too much Miller in it and too little Plato. I had read in
that course nothing but Plato and was trying to "follow
the argument," Plato's argument, trying to make it come
alive on Plato's terms. I was not in it at all—except as the
present actuality of Plato, as someone moved by those
arguments. If Plato did not come alive in me, then he was
no living force at all. That was a troublesome, if vague,
realization at the time. But it was a factor in my eventual
claim that philosophy was its own *history,* and that the eva-
sion of the present was a reduction of history to what was
itself never a presence. A teacher of poetry not *now* moved
by the poem, not presenting its force in his own words,
has not shown what was ever alive in the poem itself. But
this is a peculiarity of *all* humanities. They cannot be
"taught," as geometry can be taught, the teacher never
appearing in what he says.

And yet, even in geometry, the force of the teaching
derives from a manifest engagement of the teacher in the
discourse. I was fortunate to have had one such teacher in
high school. She *was* geometry, as my algebra teacher was
not algebra. In that sense not even geometry can be taught.

If Plato is not present in the teacher, where do you look
for him? He becomes a "thing in itself," a person or doctrine discontinuous with any this-here-now. Humanists
have been seduced by the prestige of the nonpersonal universal; they do not know that presence, the here-and-now,
is *also* a universal; nay more, that without the here-and-
now, the nonpersonal universal becomes irrelevant, as is
now being said.

So, while I must regard behaviorism on its own premises as nonsense, I must also see in it an attempt to *restore the particular* as a control and as a universal. Nothing is a stimulus that is not a meaning, and nothing is a meaning that is not a control of functioning in process. Whatever one identifies is now, has been, and will be operative as a stimulus. There is no "class" of stimuli, as there is a "class" of white swans.

For the behaviorist, a stimulus is a contrivance. One could here make an *argumentum ad hominem* about "the contriving behaviorist." I let it go in order to focus on the stimulus itself. In his view of the universal the behaviorist finds no stimulus, no here-and-now, no action—*therefore* no presence, no particular, no person. But what if the non-personal universal is itself the form of functioning, as I declare? And what if this universal is itself the order of particulars, both coming to clarity *together,* as I declare? Allow no *constitutional* place for particulars and then they become miraculous and unintelligible. But we ought not to blame behaviorists too much. In the history of Western accounts of a world the particular and finite has had no standing comparable to the universals which are never here and now. Particulars have resulted in atomism, as with the radical empiricists and with the anarchic Russell. That the particular is a constitutional universal has not been widely said—to put it conservatively.

Of course, all this is a corollary of the midworld. It is a consequence of utterances. The stimulus as a "meaning" is neither in a nonpersonal nature nor in the psychological stream of consciousness. It is actual, not "real," not "apparent." Both nature and the self are exhibited and distinguished only in the midworld.

The allure of behaviorism occurs in its restoration of the particular event, an event not to be accounted for in physics or mathematics. What is called "conditioning" is a way of explaining an event without nullifying its particularity. But since the particular is not considered constitutional, it appears as a vagrant. There is no reason for it. Quite so. I say that there is indeed no *reason* for particulars, any more than for nonpersonal universals. I say that reason is a consequence of functioning, of actuality, its self-declared presence.

If you pry a man loose from his acts, you are left with neither man nor act, nor does there remain even that distinction. For the distinction is the actual utterance and appears nowhere else under the heavens.

If the business of learning is not to give authority to the learner what is its business? But such present organization is resisted. If "learning" is illustrated in the animal laboratory, what is to stop the desperate dissent of the nullified learner? Having nullified us, the behaviorist now proposes to take charge of us. The nullifier becomes the authority. It is worth noting the parallelism between protest, dissent, riot, violence, and the spread of a view of learning in which nobody is in charge of his acts, where anyone who claims to be in charge of others is a fascist and anyone who is in charge of himself is a fool or a vain philosopher. Well, the dice of the gods are always loaded.

In summary:

(1) The purpose of these remarks is *to rescue the "stimulus."* It does no good simply to reject or attack behaviorism; one needs to find a validity in it.

(2) The stimulus is the particular.

(3) Particularity is a constitutional universal.

(4) Particularity and meaning are allied.

(5) Stimulus and response are allied and not miraculous co-variances, because both occur in the continuum of functioning. They are actualities, not realities or appearances.

(6) The actual appears as the midworld, as the immediacies that mediate between subject and object.

(7) The midworld is the utterance in which all control is exercised, as in math and logic, clocks, words, monuments, and the "meaningful" particular.

11

The Behavioral View of Action

That man is a machine has of course been proposed before. The idea is associated with La Mettrie—first half of the eighteenth century. It does not surprise to learn that he was a physician. A physician treats the *body* with *bodily* means. Whether the order of physical objects presents us with a "machine" is a question. Certainly nature is a regularity. It always was, long before Newton. There is nothing haphazard in Aristotle's "entelechy." But it was not a machine.

A machine lacks the neutrality of nature. The cotton gin cleaned cotton but did not saw logs. Nature is not a "tool" or an instrument for a specific result. The *Book of Genesis* does not suggest that the Creator had a specific end in view in projecting the world. Nature was as absolute as God, and it was no instrument that better achieved a specific result. God was not a cotton merchant or a Connecticut Yankee.

The analogy of nature with a machine is not supported by physics. The order of nature is not an adjective, a property of a *prior* object. Nature and its order are inseparable. Nature *appeared* as order. No one said, *"There* is nature, and upon examination, we find it quite orderly." As nonpersonal order there was no nature in the animistic age. Nature is not adjectivally qualified. There was a problem about the adjectives of God, and none was appropriate because any was limiting. So too with nature. The "categories" do not apply to nature. It is not red or blue (quality); here or there (space); now or then (time). Its condition is not the result of circumstances, that is, a consequence of a "cause." Nature is without limit and so has no adjectival restrictions.

But a machine is necessarily limited. Its effects are specific. It has adjectives—wooden, iron, large, small, mechanical, electrical. It can get out of order. It is not absolute. Nature is never "out of order." No object regarded as part of nature is a machine. The orderly changes that are identical with nature are of course regular, but *not* mechanical. It seems to me that there has here been a lapse in our location of the mechanical. The contrast "mechanism and vitalism" was common in my school days and has persisted. But the proper contrast is, rather, *"machine and nature."* Vitalism underlies that distinction and is its author. A machine is made and kept "in order" by a mechanic. The scientist is no mechanic; he does not keep nature in running order. When a machine breaks down it shows that, as a machine, it was no part of nature. It is thrown on a junk pile and rusts or rots. Nor is nature analogous to a machine. Nature is an infinity; a machine is particular. Nature is no object; a machine can become an object, a part of nature.

Mechanisms are specific; they do one thing, not another. Nature has no specific consequences. A machine is a design; it requires a purpose. Nature is no design, made one way rather than another; no infinity has the properties of a design. The "argument from design" broke down in the degree that nature's infinity became inherent. So long as nature was regarded as finite the design argument was proper. Kant was assailed for rejecting it, and his basic reason was that nature had no *limits* in its order.

Well, all this has a bearing on B. F. Skinner and on the condition of those who find him credible. Skinner attracts in his denials rather than his affirmations, in the denial of a psychic control in what used to be called "action" and is now called "behavior." This denial is made plausible because the psychic has been exorcised from *within* nature. Nobody today explains events in nature as resultants of purpose-control. Such purpose-control is found neither in nature nor beyond nature in the supernatural.

But why not in the supernatural? And why was a supernatural control of events in nature ever plausible, not only plausible but widely accepted? The reason was that nature was regarded as an object and finite. Even Aristotle's world was finite in space, although not in time. The creation story of Jews and Christians assumed a finite nature. The gods lost power in the degree that nature lost the status of object and of finitude. This change is mostly attributable to modern science, and came about slowly. It was a consequence of the sort of account given of the changes in objects. They changed in terms of orders that *had no limits*. For example, science boasts of being "quantitative" and "exact" in terms of quantity. And such quantity was expressed in terms of orders, not of perceptions, in terms of space, time, and motion, perhaps of atoms, themselves not objects of perception but merely "units of account" as the economists say of "paper-gold."

Science exorcised purpose-control because it was not dealing with objects at all. It was not because, like common sense, it dealt with stones or the moon and could tell about them in the absence of any man's action. Indeed, the pragmatists remind us that there is no "truth" about stones unless you handle them. So, what happened was in the cards. The pragmatists became "pluralists." They lost nature as an infinite order. James proposed a finite God, quite reasonably, on the premises. The definite article became indefinable. The expression "the universe" had to go. John Dewey was reluctant to abandon scientific nature, although a pragmatist and instrumentalist. But he was in a jam. He could not get back to nature without invoking nonpragmatic action. He did not want to abandon mathematics and physics, both of which are infinities and butter no parsnips. In math there are no parsnips, nor butter either.

The fulcrum here is that people did not know *why* purpose-control had been exorcised from nature. They said it had been. Only a dunce would allege purpose-control in the motions of the moon or the eruption of a volcano. But physics is not "about" the moon as a particular object. The moon could explode and not disconcert the physicist. Such explosions do occur and get enclosed in a wholly general account of order.

Where, then, is one to find a place for the story told by Skinner? Not in nature as disclosed in mathematics and physics, supplemented by hypotheses (a logical form). All you get there is universals such as $S = \frac{1}{2} gt^2$. No change in physics has a local cause; every change fades away into a universal order. Is Skinner proposing to relegate the pecking of pigeons to the same universal uniformities as occur in physics, where there are no intervening purposes?

There is no tampering with the inexorable processes of the physical world. You cannot get water to boil by blowing a whistle or ringing a bell. You need a fire or some other mode of raising temperature. In physics there are no circumventions. Water is what becomes of it, and what becomes of it is what it is. Water is never deflected from its "natural" ways. It is not subject to "conditioning." Physics repudiates conditioning. Admit conditioning, and physics would collapse.

A physicist can boil a kettle of water in the kitchen, and Skinner can get a pigeon to peck, but the basis of the two results have nothing in common. What is the universal order that sees the pecking of pigeons as part of a continuum of change? For the physicist that continuum is the *same* as nature. That is because physics is concerned not with local changes but with a universal order. Whatever a physicist says is in terms of yardsticks, clocks, balances, numbers, or other "units of account," none of which is an object in nature. Those pigeons of B. F. Skinner are *not objects in the physical universe.*

The pecking of pigeons is not accounted for in terms of any "unit of account" that projects a universal order, an infinity.

Now, I have no doubt that a pigeon can be treated as a scientific object. But I can find no instance in physics or chemistry of a change attributed to a "stimulus." Nothing "stimulates" the solar system. Any change in it falls back on an order with which it is even now continuous. No new influence plays upon it. It is part of a wider order, and any "prediction" about it is based solely on *what it is now*. The pigeon, with a "nervous system," can be treated as part of the same nature as the solar system. In that case no change in the pigeon is any more attributable to a stimulus than is a change in the solar system.

It isn't so much that I want to find flaws in Skinner. It is, rather, that I do not propose to abandon Newton, Avogadro, or Einstein. I have very basic reasons for clinging to nature as a region of uniformity and infinity. Science projects that region. It was a long and rather awesome process. That pigeon does not belong there. Nothing said about it projects the universal order that is the essential glory of science. Pigeons do not define a universe, but numbers and yardsticks do. And they are not perceptual objects. They are "functioning objects" or "units of account," or formalities, or actualities.

Skinner should quarrel with physicists before he quarrels with philosophers. I don't notice that some eminent physicist hails Skinner as a contributor to our knowledge of physical nature, bringing the sort of clarification supplied by a Dalton, Laviosier, or Hertz.

Skinner is a sort of magician. You have probably seen a chemist giving an exhibition of wonders. He pours something from a beaker into a test tube, shakes it, heats it, and, presto, there is a brilliant blue color, perhaps a delicious or repulsive odor, a flame, an erupting cloud of smoke. Wonderful! Up to a point, the chemist is pleased but he has no respect for anyone who does not understand the structure of—perhaps—the sulphuric acid that he poured into the test tube. It is all clear enough to him. The acid resulted in exactly what it was defined as surely producing, given molecules, atoms, atomic weights, valences, or other factors that, chemically, *are* that acid. He is no wizard. But it is not Skinner's claim that he merely shows the nature of a pigeon so that any change in the bird exemplifies a general order of change.

I would like to know about that pigeon. It is no part of nature as presented in physics. Nor for Skinner is it an "animate" object with some sort of "mind" or "soul" and so to be understood in terms of psychic faculties. It isn't really "free." It may feel so, but that is an illusion. Skinner is not interfering with the pigeon's freedom or with yours or mine, when he proposes to train us in new ways of behaving. We are not now "free." There is no such interference possible.

Nor do I suppose that the pigeon is an item in Skinner's stream of consciousness—a term not recognized by him. There are three possible locations of that pigeon: it fits into none of them. The problem shifts from Skinner to the pigeon. What is that famous bird? There is the crux. Whatever is said "about" the pigeon will be controlled by the manner of *identifying* it. What is that manner? I'm beginning to doubt that Skinner has any pigeon.

It may be a bit technical, and so not effective in dealing with Skinner and his admirers, to note that talking "about" requires a prior identification of the object. What one says "about" it follows the identification. What is one to say "about" the universe when one cannot first produce it as an object? "What are you talking 'about'?" has seemed a fair question. But it turns out that one cannot talk "about" the universe or "about" God. They are not items in an environment. I would suggest that the ancient and enduring idea of substance conveys this assumption that talk must be "about" something. A declarative sentence needs a subject of discourse. A predicate is "about" a subject. One asks questions about a subject. Are all swans white? No use asking unless one has identified what one is asking "about."

All that seems a bit stuffy, but it is quite in point if one says that one is now to make professional talk "about" pigeons. Everyone seems to take it for granted, as quite obvious, that one can, of course, talk about this pigeon.

There is the bird; now let's see what can be said about it. All that seems quite in line with common sense.

If one does talk "about," one assumes some status for the substantive. What one then says is controlled by the setting that has identified the object. One can ask "how many" pigeons; "how much" one weighs; "when" it eats; to "what species" it belongs, and the like. Or, who discovered pigeons? What colors have they? One *comes upon* them, or upon anything else that one talks about. They are not miraculous revelations, absolute "data," quite without a place in a continuity; about such discrete absolutes there is nothing to say; no predicate is suitable *or* unsuitable.

So, I ask, how does Skinner come upon a pigeon? If he sees it, is a pigeon nothing but a seeing, so that it would not appear as *not* an eagle or as *not* a fish found in water? What it is "not" is no optical datum.

But if one talks about pigeons, one talks in a certain way. For Skinner this is not the way a physicist or chemist talks. They do not talk about birds, but not about the moon. Nor does Skinner talk as if the bird were animate, with an animal "soul" that controlled and launched its acts or behavior. Nor does he talk about a person as if his prior identification was in terms of a rational soul or mind or spirit. Nor does he present himself in such prior identification.

My conclusion is that Skinner cannot, does not, exhibit what he is talking about.

Further, he must resist all attempts to say what he is talking about. For that would give prior status to a setting in terms of which statements "about" pigeons would be controlled. What that setting might be remains obscure— not physical, animistic, theological, logical, mathematical. To talk "about" is to talk in one of those ways of talking.

Further, there is no prior way of talking. That there is talk at all, or what is so called, is for him a wholly accidental discovery. This is the correlative of the absence of that prior setting mentioned above. Such a setting appears only in a discourse—physics, for example. It is not even a resultant of some prior and assumed order, physical, theological, psychic. It is not to be controlled by logic. Logic gives utterance a status not purely accidental. "Accident" is itself a logical term. Talk is neither controlled by a prior setting announced by a discourse nor has it a structure of its own—logic, for example.

So, Skinner cannot say, "Let us now talk about pigeons." No way of such talk is either allowed or required. The pigeon is not *identified* in a discourse; *therefore* no discourse is extended apropos of pigeons.

Whatever Skinner is talking about he cannot say. If a pigeon is to be talked about, there is a prior talk in identifying the bird. Skinner has no prior talk, and so no prior setting or order; for such a setting occurs in a discourse. I would say—do say—it occurs *only* as discourse. For I regard utterance as ontological and constitutional. Short of that I see no way of avoiding Skinner's anarchy. I say that space is the projection of a yardstick, which is no object of perception yet requires bodily functioning—seeing, handling, counting. I want the actual. If order is not actual, it fades away. I deny that one could even fall back on the psychology of the empiricists. The psychological is itself a distinction generated by the pure act, as when one counts or measures and so can make mistakes and say what is not so, which is what cannot be *said* if one is to present oneself or any object.

The instructive disclosure of Skinner occurs in the loss of all presence, that is, of the actual. He is forcing us to revise our metaphysics. I can talk "about" as well as the next man, but only if talk is not *subsequent* to what it is about. I deny the whole psychology of "perception" that says in consequence of a "stimulus" I see the maple tree in my front yard. I see no maple tree until I have a name for it and so can "see" a not-oak tree, although the not-oak tree is no perception.

We have struggled to get at a "truth" that is prior to any utterance about it. We are to keep out. Do not appear in whatever you say is so. On that basis no one can appear. If all I say is a resultant, I cannot name or describe that prior cause. That is why Skinner cannot produce a pigeon as something to be talked about. It isn't that he finds no logic in the cooing or pecking; it is that he has no pigeon—*this-here-now* bird, *one* bird, and so forth.

I reduce the problem, then, to the simple statement: "Skinner has no pigeon." But neither do those whom he baffles, while also attracting them. They are lost in a confusion, in an anarchy. For Skinner, the pigeon and what then appears is an *absolute phenomenon*.

It is notorious that order is never found among phenomena. But on what basis could even that discrimination be made? I say, of course, that order is the form of act. No talking, no logic. It is an inherent form of the actual, not the only one.

The actual, that is, the midworld, carries one down to the present as functioning. It makes any composition historical. It is the immediacy that projects infinity. I can give no "reason" for counting, and so forth. Reason inheres in such actualities.

12

The Stimulus as Potential

I have used the word "meaning," not a word I like. It suggests a definition, as in a dictionary. If one asks, "What does it mean?" one is asking what to *do* about an appearance. This is caused by some stoppage of action or of "response," by the failure of an appearance to operate as a "stimulus."

An appearance can have a meaning, although one may do nothing. A shrill whistle is heard six times; what does it "mean"? It means a fire at the corner of Main and Elm. I may not go to see it, or to assist in putting it out, but I might. A response peculiar to that appearance is possible.

For any person at a place and time most appearances of that sort are ignored. They are "meanings" and so recognized but are not now in the course of action.

This suggests that any "stimulus" is a "potential" and that there are multitudes of potential stimuli or meanings, few of which are now influences, or controls, of present action.

This potentiality seems to me important. How is one to say that a fire whistle, a word, a clock, a monument is a "stimulus" when it is *not now* producing a response? Does it then cease to rate as a stimulus? Lacking a present response, how can one allege any stimulus? Yet many objects of the sort I call functioning objects continue as known potential stimuli. Words in a dictionary, some of them rarely used, or never used by me, get recognized as stimuli, as occasions of response.

There seems, in short, to be a whole world of such potential stimuli. These are all functioning objects, what I call the midworld. They are all "meanings." All provoke and regulate response.

An object in nature has no potential. It never fails to be all that it is. Whatever gravitational force the earth may have upon the moon is *constantly* effective. It is true that wood can burn and water boil; but one is not therefore claiming that the water in the kettle at room temperature is other than it might now be. That it *not* boil at room temperature is part of its identification as water.

The uniformity of nature—as in a formula—expresses the invariance of an object, of all objects as identified. Whatever boils at room temperature at sea level is not water.

Nature has no "potential"; it has only change in accordance with the constant identity of the changing object.

In contrast, a meaning or stimulus has no such constancy. Treat a yardstick as a piece of wood and it no longer provokes the process of measurement on various occasions. I have here several yardsticks; they rarely exert the consequences of that status. They are potential. They are functioning objects. They are in the midworld, not in nature. Nor are they "data" to a passive stream of consciousness. They are actualities, not realities or appearances. On their terms we determine what is "really" the length of the room and what is its "apparent" length. The room has *neither* a real *nor* an apparent length without that intermediary. The long debate over appearance and reality had no middle term, no common ground. This is supplied by the peculiar sort of object that is also a meaning. There is no yardstick, word, monument, or whistle that "has" a meaning; it *is* a meaning. Objects in nature produce no specific consequence because they lack the status of a meaning. They are not actual in their particularity.

To identify a meaning or a stimulus is not to identify an object as a constant. *No object is a stimulus.* This simple declarative sentence tells what is amiss and confusing in behavioral science.

The potential status of the stimulus is evidence that it is not an object in nature.

There is no science of the potential. There is no science of the words in the dictionary. All are functioning objects. All are operative only on occasion; all change their meaning as they support or confuse an occasion and the act that marks an occasion. Every word is the evidence and actuality of a local and particular event.

Any word or other functioning object is a potential stimulus. In nature there is neither such potentiality nor any stimulus. The Parthenon is a stimulus. Barbarians see it as an object and would use its marble to make lime. Other barbarians use words for similarly desirable purposes.

The functioning object is the appearing of the act. People say that they find no act. They are the same people who find no "stimulus" but only objects that produce no "response."

The stimulus is a potential for local and particular events. It is only the potential that is both the manifestation of an act and *therefore* its control. There is no science that tells what a person who reads, who sees a monument, who tells time by the clock, will be doing. The reason is that all such functioning objects are themselves in their status and appearance, the particular consequences of a particular doing, of a here-and-now, of the actual.

What is to become of me once I read? Nobody knows. A scientist, perhaps, a poet, a philosopher, yes, even a behaviorist who cannot say what he is talking about or that he is talking at all.

A potential is also a potency. In nature there is no potency. Nothing there can become what it is not already. Nature as described by science manifests no power. Nothing there is to be ascribed to a power. Such control has been exorcised. Even causality, with its suggestion of enforcement or influence, has been declared a "pseudo-concept." On the premises rightly so. In passivity no cause is discovered. (Years ago I wrote a paper ["The Paradox of

Cause"] on the interdependence of cause and purpose, that is, on the local control that generates *both* causes and purposes.)

The idea of power is now decried. Power is said to be arbitrary, fascist, dogmatic, and so on. The case for power is worse than that on premises that do not recognize the midworld and the functioning object. The case is worse because it is then utter nonsense. A world that is not the manifestation of power does not contain dunces or villains. "Doing what comes naturally" is no doing.

If you say of a man that he has great potentialities, you are not treating him as an object in nature. He has potential only in so far as he is seen responsive to power. Perhaps he has potential as a mathematician. If so, it is in his responsiveness to numbers. They express and manifest a power. They command in terms of their inherent power. Is a man a "square" because he finds stimulation in Pythagoras, Descartes, Leibnitz?

To be human is to find stimuli in the midworld. But such power is also discipline. A word is a danger. Any actuality is a risk because it is also a presence, a here-and-now, the declaration of a local control that, in its formal consequences, also declares a world.

The reason for the current disrepute of metaphysics is very simple. It is that no local control is allowed. It is not allowed because the basis of such control—the functioning actuality—has not been recognized. Treat the midworld as an object or as an item in the stream of consciousness, and the humanities are lost.

I stay with the point: there are no stimuli except in the efficacy of a functioning object. There is no other efficacy. There is no other potential. Every functioning object is a power. It is the stimulus to the particular event. Apart from that the stimulus becomes an affront to science.

I would save the authority of science and of the nature it has disclosed in its vast continuum. Nature so disclosed is the form of functioning. It is the consequence of local control. It is the consequence of actualities such as numbers, words, yardsticks, and clocks. Nature is the consequence of those commanding stimuli that appear as actualities, not as objects or content of consciousness. To revert to the simplest example, the yardstick is an actuality. It is both the consequence and the further stimulus to functioning. It is an arduous command, and it led to questions about the synchronization of clocks in a Euclidean order of space. Who the deuce is Einstein with no yardstick? And no clock? And no numbers?

It is not the midworld that is hazy; the haze clouds whatever is alleged in its nonrecognition. Nature itself becomes a haze and "life, like a dome of many-colored glass, stains the white radiance of eternity." But if Shelley had accounted for glass, domes, colors, for life itself, he would not have written those despairing lines. A poet, above all men, should avow the power of the word. Without the actual word we would not have that eloquent line any more than $E = MC^2$. There is Shelley. He spoke. But I am not allowing anyone to allege that "this is a piece of glass" unless he accepts the potency of the utterance. The Greeks were smart; they "had a word for it." It was very great in Plato that he wondered about the "right" word, even though he could not solve the problem on his premises.

In the caves of the Pyrenees there are drawings of a herd of deer. A friend of mine, a lawyer, who saw them, gave me a quiet but stirring account of his visit. What was it that he saw? Deer? A pretty picture? That would not have prompted his words or his manner. Nor was he commenting on the degree of intelligence of Neanderthal man. It was, rather, that in those caves something was revealed. Here was a voice, an utterance, an announcement, not of any matter of fact, but of the *presence* of men and objects. Those drawings were a voice.

Out of the silence a voice, out of the darkness a light. In the story of chaos from which the world emerged it was the generation of particulars—earth, sky, vegetation—that brought content and form. I think my friend felt that he was a spectator of the creation. On what other basis could one find anything awesome in those drawings? The maker, the poet, saw himself in telling what he saw. He is not represented there, but presented.

This is the midworld. It does not represent, it *presents*. The person "appears" in the same utterance that declares that objects have appeared. The drawings say nothing about the general cosmos; they say that the hunter is a hunter of deer, an observer of their ways, a discriminator of objects allied to his functioning. Those drawings are the original school book. Children could learn from them. Attention is directed, and only so is discovered. They are the first identifiable stimulus, the particular that is continuous with other particular events, directing what is seen, where one goes, what one does. The drawing is a power, not another item of a passive consciousness that has no center and no control and is a chaos without focus, without arrest. The drawing is also a potential. There are other drawings, of bison. Will one today hunt the deer or the bison? Because this stimulus is an actuality it is also a potential, like any word in the dictionary. To "respond" to a dictionary is to find a stimulus in a particular word, not in the totality of all words, an illusion dispelled so soon as any word is uttered and so modified in its appearance, making more work for the lexicographer.

I don't say that an examination of the stimulus is the only way to discovering the actual and the midworld. I started with history as a curious discourse that had not a word to say for itself in terms of the controls of science, easily the most authoritative and prestigious account of nature and man. But in nature there is no Mediaeval mind, no Dante, no Chartres, and it is such peculiar objects that are the subject matter of history. So I come to the midworld on which science itself is wholly dependent for its proclaimed rigors and truth.

The stimulus is a most interesting idea because it is so persistent and at the same time absurd on behavioral premises. The more I looked at it the more I was drawn to the status of the particular and the price to be paid for allowing it any efficacy. In so far as I have located it, the control has been in terms of the as yet unacknowledged actuality of the midworld.

Put broadly, if one wants civilization and civility, where does one look if not to the revelations of utterance? And where else is that inherent discipline that is also our freedom?

The chaos of today is the historical consequence of a metaphysical lapse. But it is historic and fateful, as is any historical identity. That today quite stupid people search for their identity is a consequence of the account of the world that the learned propagate. For them the actual has no authority and rates no reverence because it is not recognized. They brush it aside. The lord and master is revealed as impotent. Of course it is the other fellow's impotence that allures the critics. They are hot on the trail of any pretension to authority. They allow no presence. They are beginning to see that what is sauce for the goose is also the flavor of the gander. But for the present one has no chance of making any man equivalent to his word or utterance of any sort. Physics, psychology, and theology are still too powerful. So we slip from the totalitarian to the chaotic. And then comes the behaviorist, who does not like the chaos and wants to take charge of it. And it is not without interest that the media for all their clamorous demand to be "free" give an attentive ear to this social engineer. They don't really like Caliban.

13

Adjustment in Psychiatry

There are no maladjustments in physics, or in nature viewed physically. Earthquakes, volcanos, parasites, diseases, are merely part of nature's processes. Physical nature is lawful; these laws always operate; they operate upon all objects of physics; they cannot cease to operate, because such operations define the object of physical nature. Death from typhoid is no maladjustment of physical nature, but only one factor in its changes, laws, objects, or properties. The idea of maladjustment has no place in physical nature. That is a confusion of categories, as if one were to speak of a heavy triangle, or a $\sqrt{-2}$ with a velocity of 60 m.p.h.

Adjustment refers to some relation involving purpose rather than cause. It suggests sufficiency, satisfaction, success, and their opposites. One may adjust the carburetor or the spark plug points. In doing so one implies no lapse of physical law. If the points of a spark plug open too far, the spark doesn't jump at a given voltage, nor ought it to jump at that voltage. Spark plugs are reliable only because some openings are too wide for a given voltage; for this permits control of the right space for a given voltage. But if one wishes the auto to run, then the points need to be "adjusted." The points are "correctly" adjusted in terms of a wish or purpose. One might, however, prevent theft of an auto by removing a few plugs and spreading the points. Then the points would be "adjusted," quite as truly as in the former case. Thus, *no state of affairs among objects in their physical relations suggests either adjustment or maladjustment.* A purpose is necessary.

A purpose is not a change among objects viewed physically. No theory of adjustment occurs in terms of the laws or observations of physics. A nonphysical ingredient is necessary to give the term "adjustment" denotation. *Physics does not define purpose, hence not maladjustment or adjustment.*

Purpose, however, defines an activity. In nature as physical there is no activity. Neither is there passivity. There is only lawful change, or events, or things. There is no identity except as lawful change. There are no accidents, because all events are viewed as ideally conditioned, never free from condition, never free from an endless complex of condition. No event is an entity in itself; hence none can passively receive influences. Every stage of every object or event is through and through defined in circumstance. There is nothing outside of circumstance that circumstance can invade or can invade circumstance. Thus, physical nature is neither active nor passive. *Only in the context of purpose is either activity or passivity definable.*

It would seem reasonable at this point to look for purpose as well as for activity and passivity in a region dissociated from nature. But there are reasons against this. The first is simple and would be generally accepted: namely, *no purpose is separable from physical order.* Ignorance of nature prevents purpose, and disorder in nature prevents purpose. The second reason, less likely of acceptance, is this: *nature—as physical—cannot be defined without purpose.* The general evidence for this rests on voluntaristic philosophies such as experimentalism or pragmatism. The order of nature is discovered only in an active examination of nature. Ask no questions, and there are no answers. At any stage in the history of knowledge, nature is defined in terms of the sort of questions asked to account for its changes. Thus, we ask causal questions and say that nature is causal. But causal questions are rather recent. Or, very lately, the causal axiom has been doubted, and so nature becomes a matter of statistical frequencies. But, in general, *it seems not possible to find the factor of purpose, hence of activity, passivity, and adjustment either in nature alone or in purpose alone.*

If maladjustment requires both purpose and physics, it seems not an altogether technical sort of relation. One may say that the relation of purpose to nature has two aspects: (1) the aspect of technique and (2) the aspect of organism.

The aspect of technique is the specific approach to nature. A bit of thread on the tip of my pen prevents making these notes with the desired clarity. So I may take time to remove the thread. This sort of situation occurs as a universal property of purpose. One acts when some situation is not quite manageable, and so one encounters everywhere the need of observation, caution, and theory. This situation leaves the purpose quite sound and healthy. To object to technical obstacles is in effect to object to nature itself. One is not maladjusted to nature in principle because there are obstacles, or difficulties, or retardation in completing purposes in detail. Nor is one maladjusted to nature because one dies. This needs fuller defense, but for brevity's sake I will merely say that finite purposes define their own inadequacy in the face of the situation that makes them possible, namely an infinite nature that can never be mastered in all detail. On the other side the infinitude of nature is itself the reflection of finite purposes and could not otherwise be discovered. Nowadays we all take the infinitude of nature for granted. But it was not always so. This conviction had to wait for the development of purpose and, especially, for the purposes of the experimental scientist. His act defines its own eternal incompleteness. But before nature was infinite there was a supernatural infinitude. Wherever there is finitude, that is, purpose or personality, there is some sort of appropriate and compensating infinitude. *Technical incompleteness is not, then, in any way unusual or abnormal or diseased.* It is both purpose in principle, and nature in principle. A man is not insane when he can't make his auto run, or find the shut-off for the water pipe that leaks, or doesn't know what to do for indigestion, sunburn, or dandruff. In those respects life is just one thing after another. *To hope for adjustment to nature would then be both absurd and suicidal.*

But in getting adjusted to nature there is also the second aspect of "organism." An organic adjustment is something total, not something local and detailed. The adjustment to the spark plug is a local adjustment, but so are any number of other special acts. A man needs to adjust himself not to spark plugs, for he may not have an auto, but to a situation viewed as a whole. But this totality will not be definable in terms of any given set of specific objects or problems. It will vary with each man, and with each historical outlook. A man is adjusted in his own situation, not in that of another. A theory of adjustment, since it aims to be general, must then ignore what is specific in a totality and deal only with any possible totality.

This totality is the individual world. It is not the individual and the world. The latter conception would restore the separation that seems indefinable. *Adjustment is a wholly internal process,* not a process between the individual and "physical and social reality." Objects viewed externally call for only technical adjustment; they do not, and cannot, call for organic adjustment.

Psychological maladjustment is not definable as between an individual and an alien "physical and social reality" but only within the person or individual. Were the maladjustment a question of a relation to such an alien reality, then by changing the reality one could remove the maladjustment. For example, if one can't stand farm country because of hay fever, one can go to the north shore of Lake Superior, where there is no pollen. If one can't work in a cold room, one can build a fire or put on a sweater. But psychiatric maladjustment is not cured in this way. Sometimes a change of scene does good, but only because it can slowly effect a change in outlook. Otherwise we could soon cure insanity by moving patients from Northampton to Boston or New York. But the psychiatric maladjustment is organic. It reveals a flaw in the way a man looks at himself, at other persons, or at nature. It concerns the whole man. It is a flaw in principle not in detail.

Besides, one can't change physical reality, or any reality. Reality is not an object, like a cold room or pollen-laden air. Reality is what can't be changed. Shall one then say,

"Adjust or die"? It seems obvious that this is a most discouraging idea. Here lies one of the basic handicaps of a
therapy that promises to secure a more happy life. *An alien
reality has no claim upon one.* Nor has it any compulsion.
Unless one is defined through it, one can take it or leave it; and
only an arbitrary medicine could treat one as in any way
sick were one to turn away from it. Of course psychiatry
does not suppose one can turn away. It does not suppose
that one has that alternative open to one. We are somehow
bound to the "physical and social reality." It is not an incident in our lives, not an accident of our perceptions or of
our motivation. Yet the idea of getting into and out of
adjustment with reality suggests some status for the ego
apart from it, suggests that there are impulses that can be
defined without it, that these impulses are very strong and
can lead one into difficulty. Were this true, those antireal-
istic impulses would have their own status, their own sort
of reality. That is dualism; but it is in no way a description
of any failure to face reality, or a description of an unheal-
thy outlook. Failure to secure adjustment to this allegedly
objective "physical and social reality" is no failure at all.
Indeed, it would be no concern of one's own, or certainly
no organic concern, no concern upon which one's integrity
of mind depended. A man who would adjust himself to a
"fact," to a reality not defined in himself, would be capit-
ulating. Nature and society would then be ordering him
around. One seems offered a choice of madness or slavery.
This cannot be the answer to a distressed mind. This was
the answer of stoicism. *The human appeal of psychiatry cannot eventually lie in adjustment to a nonhuman reality.* One can
hardly blame those who prefer a different sort of absolute,
namely God. He gives one the important satisfaction of
being free to sin. God allows one to be evil, and that is a
more appealing alternative than to be mad. For one can sin
only in one's right mind.

Besides, *the idea of adjustment to "reality" is not a scientific
idea.* No object of nature reacts to "reality." Water can react
to fire, carbon to oxygen, but none of these reacts to reality. Similarly, a man may react to fire, or to oxygen, but

those are specific reactions. Such reactions go on every day and explain what we know about fire and oxygen, but they are not the type of reaction that involves the coherence, the integrity, the self-criticism of a personality. How would an object or a man get adjusted to reality? What would one do next? One can get adjusted to new millinery, but not to reality, even though one calls it "social and physical." This is not so much too big an order as a meaningless one, if one takes reality to be a fact, an object, or situation to which adjustment is to be made. In dealing organically, one needs to avoid analogy with the mechanical.

Furthermore, there is difficulty in seeing how one could ever claim that an adjustment to reality had occurred. For, reality is a constant. It is not specific and, hence, does not suggest a technical adjustment, or reaction, or response. A reaction or response is identified through some variation in the stimulus. One responds variously only to such situations as changes in temperature or to changes in light. The peculiar response needs the peculiar stimulus. The anopheles mosquito causes malaria, the stegomyia causes yellow fever. In these cases, indeed in all properly psychological responses and in all physical changes, the peculiarity of the response entails the peculiarity of the stimulus, or cause, or condition, or occasion. By varying the conditions, one varies the response, and only under such circumstances can one speak of a response to a situation. Constant factors of environment secure no specific reaction or adjustment. Response or reaction occur only through differences. They are differences; they must be understood through corresponding differences.

Now, reality is a constant. Its opposite is unreality. But can one devise a situation experimentally, or observe one empirically, where in one case the situation to be responded to is reality, and in the other case, unreality? Is this analagous to the boiling of water in the presence of heat and the freezing of water in the absence of a known degree of heat? How would one know experimentally or observationally what a person would do in the presence of reality and in the presence of unreality? The truth is that neither of these situations can be objectively, scientifically, or empirically produced. The real and the unreal are not situations—different, and definably different, situations—to which one can introduce a person in order to observe the corresponding differences of reaction or adjustment. Hence I venture to conclude that *the idea of "adjustment to reality" is not a scientific idea at all.* It is not analogous to any possible scientific type of reaction.

As a matter of fact, the normal reaction, allegedly directed upon reality, and the abnormal reaction, allegedly directed upon unreality, are both known only in themselves, only in terms of their own coherence or incoherence and never in their relation to an independently definable reality or unreality. *The only clue to the normal and abnormal, to the real and the unreal, lies in the act itself,* never in a relation of act to situation, the real situation or the unreal situation. There are not two factors, but only one; namely, the act itself, or the personality itself.

The phrase "adjustment to reality" means the wholly organic adjustment of personality to itself. It is not a technical or specific adjustment but a total adjustment. It can be found only where a mind finds itself, not where it finds or responds to, or fits itself into, something other than itself. Such statements may go counter to scientific attitudes; but it is the point of this analysis that the psychiatric problem of adjustment is not analogous to a scientific problem.

I observed further back that the problem of adjustment to nature had the two aspects of technical and organic. Psychiatric maladjustment occurs only as organic maladjustment, not as technical maladjustment. It seems, then, that all psychiatric problems occur over a failure to recognize the organic identity of nature, or the real, as being also the organic identity of the personality. *The break in this integrity of a world, or of a self, is the generic locus of conflict and of all its specific forms.*

For example, there are maladjustments due to conflict between self and society. Egoism finds itself frustrated in conformity, or even in a recognition of the lives and interests of others. There is sulkiness, retirement, nonresponsiveness, lack of cooperation. This may then involve fantasy and perhaps depression. Here occur stubbornness, fears, cruelties, impossible schemes, all a result of a negative egoism. It is now said that such a person is not facing reality, in this case social reality.

This is true enough. But what is this social reality? Such a person is not just unconscious of society. His attitude is not merely brutal, not merely ignorant. No, he is very keenly conscious of society, painfully conscious of it. But why, then, is he said to be escaping from reality? His conduct is said to be unsocial, or socially troublesome, or socially injurious. But so is a wild beast or a mosquito socially troublesome; yet the mosquito is not insane or maladjusted. It may be having the very best of times in its own way. And a tiger may curl up in deep contentment just after dining off a human victim. For a tiger he is in a most prosperous condition. Yet we regard an unsocial human being as mentally twisted, and we explore his soul to find out why.

Is it because there is some contradiction in himself? But how could that be the case unless he were trying both to have his cake and eat it too? Perhaps society is necessary to a man, not as a comfort or technical advantage but as part of his own meaning. Perhaps the reality to which he is maladjusted is defined quite by himself. Were social hostility a technical maladjustment, and not an organic maladjustment, it would involve no conflict, no loss of selfhood, no loss of vigor or of integrity. The reality to which adjustment is sought lies wholly in the requirement of personality. It is these demands of personality alone that define the real. It is in the conflict of these demands that mental illness occurs. The problem of the social nature of man has been studied in moral philosophy, and its phenomena extensively described.

The emphasis that psychiatry gives to social conflict is fully justified. Yet, society is *not* an object in which I have a *practical* interest and to which I can respond with technical success or failure. It is, rather, an inherent ingredient of the personality through which its own unique selfhood is defined, through which it becomes self-conscious, through which it secures effect and recognition and self-control. Society is the occasion of the idea of freedom.

The central contribution of abnormal psychology to the theory of man and nature is probably its discovery of conflict within the natural. But to make full use of the discovery, the conflict needs to be seen as the occasion whereby each individual discovers reality. There is not reality and then, *incidentally,* psychological conflict. *There is no account of reality possible except through the tensions of conflict.* For these disclose the profoundly definitive demands of an ego or personality. They say how he must construe his world. These are the essential compulsions.

Without conflict there is no sense of reality. Reality is not a datum, but an eventuality. The aim of psychiatry should be to exploit conflict to secure reality, not to secure adjustment to a postulated reality. The postulation of reality makes conflict either an aberration or else part of the real. Yet nature viewed as postulate has no aberrations. And if conflict is part of nature, then nature must be so defined as to include conflict in its own meaning.

Psychiatry must offer men freedom, or else it must present them as victims. It can offer them freedom in so far as it can capitalize on conflict, at least in theory. Psychiatry, in the concept of conflict and maladjustment, has raised up a terrible picture. The answer can be no less emancipating than the question is discouraging. It can give this answer only in so far as it views conflict not mechanistically or technically but as organic, and as the very means by which organism is discovered and identified. This is its great contribution.

The point of view that discovers biology has already undergone conflict. Biology as the domain of life can be identified only as life is self-conscious. Consciousness, as in animals, does not recognize the difference between the body and the mind, the dead and the living. These distinctions depend on self-consciousness and, hence, on some measure of conflict.

Conflicts occur as states of consciousness. Their *occasion* is specific and psychological. Any case record shows this. But their *meaning* is never specific. Their meaning is in the disclosure of the real, the nonpsychological, the norm. For there is no way of finding the normal except through the disclosure of these terrible forces and demands. Just so long as these are viewed as not themselves indicative of the real, the abnormal will be only a horror within a reality not molested by these aberrations. That reality will of course be itself an indefinable illusion, an empty ideal nowhere discoverable. The normal is the organic and self-possessed. It is functional integrity.

For over a century there has been prominent in European and American philosophy a type of theory called voluntarism. It is in contrast with intellectualism. The chiefly known form of voluntarism in America is pragmatism. This view defines truth as a consequence of action. Truth is to be found by experiment and as an answer to needs and questions, rather than by passive reception of data and their intellectual fabrication. But the truths that pragmatism promises are all specific truths, if that be a possible qualification of truth. What it tries to avoid is universal truths, and for the excellent reason that universal truths are not, and cannot be, experimental. Not being experimental they are viewed as not human in meaning or utility. The real is, then, for the pragmatist without universal or necessary character, excepting the single general property of being always verified in some specific experiment that makes a specific difference in experience. Here is a voluntaristic view of the real. But it is not an organic view. Pragmatism sees the real as definable only in the context of action; but the action is always specific, as are also the true and the real.

Psychiatry, in contrast, speaks of nonspecific and nonscientific adjustments. The problems of pragmatism are all technological and forward looking; but the problems of psychiatry are all organic and look only to a present equilibrium. The pragmatist is a meliorist; both James and Dewey are meliorists. But the psychiatrist is dealing not in comparatives of fulfillment but in the capacity for living the moment as a whole man. The psychiatrist isn't promising a method for utilizing the energy of uranium or for making a model apartment building, with swimming pool for the young folks and shady benches for the old folks. The psychiatrist searches for another type of rapport with reality. His reality is in the immediate, not in the eventual.

This immediate reality is wholly a matter of form, not of utilities or of content. This is shown by the absence of unity or of form in the maladjusted person. Such a person is in conflict; he has repressions, fears, hysteria. His personality is marked by dissociation, not by lack of orange juice. Yet his discomforts would not occur in the absence of "drives," or of "instinct," or of "urges." There is no psychiatric maladjustment in the absence of volition. Nor is there any psychiatric maladjustment over the *specific* volition. It occurs over the form of the will, over the general properties of the complete will. *Psychiatry is the general theory of the genesis of the form of will.* And this form of the will is also the form of the *real*. It is the form of that reality with which it has been supposed the person was out of adjustment. Hence, reality is individual; it is social; and it is physical. For these are ingredients in the completeness of will and of action.

It is a fact, and it ought to be a fact, that men have always hypostatized the authoritative or the ideal. Thus, the moral or religious law is given the authority of the Sinaitic God. There are many examples of this tendency. So too the psychiatrists have offered *a reality not defined within the processes of thought*. Hence they speak of getting adjusted to it, as if reality were like a hot climate, or the swaying motion of a camel. But reality is not an object. It is a wholly general idea, the most general possible. What would one expect to say about this supreme generality if not that its unity was that of form? And where could one encounter that form and the defects of its apprehension except *in the violent disorganization of an outlook?*

Psychiatry wants objectivity in the sense of something not imaginary, fantastic, or psychological. It urges acknowledgment of this nonsubjective world. Yet the form of the will is precisely what the will cannot dodge. And it is the only thing it cannot dodge. Hence, the impersonal is only the form of the personal.

Such a view is also of help in explaining the *genesis* of various patterns of culture, namely different ways in which the form of will has been historically conceived. Pioneers are likely to be queer. They are queer to others, and they are persons once in turmoil with themselves. But out of that turmoil develops a new dimension of personality, such as the idea of the individual soul, or of a causal nature through which action and intellectual integrity are possible.

To see the psychiatric in this way is to give insight to the historian, the anthropologist, and the philosopher. *A true "field theory" should be a genetic theory,* especially in psychiatry, where the factor of time is essential.

In sum, we become adjusted to reality in so far as we can identify and relate the factors of personality essential to action. These are also the form of the real. The pragmatist is the voluntarist who studies only the specific and technical side of volition. The psychiatrist is the voluntarist who studies the organic and definitive aspect of volition. The pragmatist shows the role of volition in securing *specific* truth or reality; the psychiatrist shows the role of volition in the definition of the *general form* of reality. For both, the real is inseparable from action. Neither adopts a passive or intellectualistic position. For both, the real appears in the context of urges or needs. But the needs that psychiatry studies are the general, or universal, or definitive needs. That seems to me what is true and what is false in the idea of adjustment to "physical and social reality."

14

Purpose

There is no mechanical world. There is a mechanical aspect in any world, that is, the order of the impersonal content of all worlds. This is no more than to say that all objects are mechanical. Indeed, one way of making sure that an experience concerns an object is to see whether it fits into the region of the impersonal and mechanical. If not, one has an illusion.

Accordingly, I feel that purpose is not so much an event *within* the mechanical world as one of the aspects of any world. It is an aspect that complements the mechanical. Through it the mechanical is disclosed. The order of objects (nature) doesn't come clear to anyone whose purposes are vague. Contrariwise, where nature's order is vague, one's purposes or acts seem random and fumbling to the naturalist. The precision of purpose can be no greater than the clarity of one's natural objects.

Purpose is "outside" mechanics. But it seems to me outside in the same way that a subject is outside a predicate, or a premise outside a conclusion, or space outside time, and so on.

There seems to me no order, neither purposive nor mechanical in its constitution, that includes both, as a room includes tables and chairs. There is one order, and this order needs *both* purpose and cause as complementary aspects or factors. But I think there is no reality called mechanism, and another called purpose. I am afraid that if these become separated, both become vague. I can find no "purpose" until I pitch a rock; and no rock until I pitch it, or bite it, or scatch it, or try to burn it, and so on.

The complementary relation of purpose and cause as factors of a world express life, not logic. Both have emerged from a single matrix, both have been vague in the past. It is a mistake to suppose that early man saw the world as purpose. True, he did not see it as mechanical, but neither did he see it as the outcome of action controlled by the known order (mechanical order) or environment. Early man operated through wish fulfillment, but not through purpose. Purpose modified a condition of objects and only indirectly a condition of mind; wish fulfillment seeks a modification of states of mind, but not necessarily of objects. My *purpose* is satisfied when, for example, I get the fuzz off the pen point, permitting me to write. My satisfaction is circuitous through the object and its properties. But were I to mutter an incantation I would disclose that my goal was a state of mind apart from objects. But then, I might take to thought transference, saving myself all dealing with pen and paper and spelling.

This seems to me a useful distinction, especially in psychiatry, where the environment (nature) gets lost. It also brings out the fact that dementia is not maladjustment of a technical sort, not clumsiness, but rather a failure of another sort, namely the nonrecognition of the distinction between wish and purpose. The trouble with dementia is precisely that the patient has no purpose. Therapy restores the possibility of purpose.

The urge that leads to the discovery of the difference between purpose and mechanism, and to the analysis of the properties of both, is something superior to specific purpose, that is, more basic and more inclusive. It is a phase of the unconscious from which, I think, stem history and biography.

Instinct develops from this basic and unconscious vitality. I do not believe there can be any final list of instincts.

Instinct seems to me the specific mode of discovering both purpose and nature. Suppose one calls eating an instinct. Surely it is not a purpose in a sense analogous to removing fuzz from the pen point. It is blind, urgent, fumbling, and even stupid. Man gets as hungry as an animal, but he needn't be so savage about it because he has identified the urge, accepted it, and made provision for it. In doing so he learns about nature. He also learns about the instinct, what it requires, what frustrates it, and what in turn it frustrates. To satisfy an instinct is one thing; to be concerned in having it satisfied is another. Instincts specify our modes of access to nature, to objects, to the impersonal. Every instinct thus leads to a realm of law, to a love of nature and life rather than away from them toward animalism. Something new is necessary to get a person to admit his instincts and their sequel, something more than blind animalism. That, of course, is a hard problem. I think this is related to indulgence of instinct for its own sake: gluttony, for example. Here a person doesn't want to be an animal, nor does he want to see the instinct objectively, that is, as an avenue into nature and control. He wants to be animal and man at once, and that can't be.

I do not think that purpose derives its persistent persuasion from any breakdown of mechanism as an explainer of facts. Its deep hold comes from the need of maintaining the very region of facts and causes. In terms of intimate experience, there are no stones until I throw one.

There is a science of how one holds oneself, and one's world, together. I am unable to be clear on this, but I am sure that history, philosophy, and psychology are elements of that science. They are sciences described through a special sort of failure, not the technical failure of a purpose, but the more radical failure of keeping a point of view. Chaos, somehow, not technical failure, surrounds these studies. The truth is that one can't just throw stones. Not everyone can do that. It isn't that he lacks arms or muscle, but that he lacks the point of view, the personality, the philosophy, to make throwing possible. There are sciences that study the general conditions of action, that is, of extending oneself into nature. These are, paradoxically, the sciences of personality. And the reason why personality study at those levels is scouted by many is simply that they don't see what it takes to throw stones, fire guns, and so on. They think it takes only muscle and silicon or gun powder. But that isn't so. It takes something more.

I think psychology is not so much a study of facts, as a study of the breakdown of the influence of facts. The old stimulus-response psychology, supposedly confined to facts, soon broke down into behaviorism, where there was no longer any psyche, either conscious or unconscious. That is why it seems to me that without abnormal psychology, the whole science would disappear. What makes it "abnormal" is precisely the failure of the facts and the domination of an outlook that can't define the region of fact any more. But once one tries to define the region of fact one deals in instinct, purpose, drives and urges, consciousness, the unconscious, and personality.

ii

There is the feeling that the subjective can be known only through its manifestations in the mechanical world. Here lies a problem, namely the way of understanding the objective signs of the subjective. Scientific knowledge needs to be "objective."

What I think happens here is that the objective becomes equated with content, and with the order of content that is causality. That the subjective can have some other form is the obscure point. If one could be satisfied that it did have form, one would remove the dislike of it as vagrant. The subjective would acquire some security if it had shape, even if that shape were not the causal order among accidentally found objects. Causal order is not in too good repute as absolute object. There is something formal about cause itself. And I think that if one could be satisfied on that point, one could also agree to look for other sorts of order without feeling that one was abandoning restraint upon the vagrancy of the subjective.

Unfortunately, the order of the subjective, if there be any, can't very well be a property of content, or of objects. But I think it is well to admit that and have it clear. Let it be understood that no claims for purpose will be made on the basis of any discovered fact, or on the basis of any property of discovered fact. Let all the discovered facts exhibit the order of cause and never the order of purpose. Let them show no inwardness—no thought, value, conflict, error, or evil. Let them have no history, no ethics, no psychology.

Then one can urge that causes are not discovered without purpose. And on the reverse, one can urge that purposes are vague in the measure that nature is vague. Ignorance of nature is also confusion of purpose. Lack of purpose means ignorance of nature.

That is not enough, though good so far as it goes. One needs to know how the distinction of purpose and cause is made. If one is ready to put some meaning into purpose, the above argument has some force. But the mechanist, or the scientist as mechanist, can always claim that he does not grant the distinction on which the argument is based. There is something arbitrary about it from his point of view.

In normal psychology this distinction is assumed. Even McDougall, with his "seven marks of behavior," has to assume that the reader understands the idea of purpose in order to show that behavior manifests purpose. But normal psychology has never been at ease on this point. In olden days it accepted parallelism; more recently it has been inclined toward mechanism. Purpose has remained a dogma. Now of course it is true that causality is no less a dogma. But that is not persuasive to the man whose dogma seems to him the very mode of order and responsible statement. (Incidentally, all dogma has that quality to the mind that entertains it. Dogma is always an essay in order.)

If all psychology were reducible to learning, I do not

think that purpose could be defended. Learning becomes "conditioning," attributable to environment. It lacks the necessary inwardness of purpose. Learning tends to be a natural and objective property of some parts of nature. And in general I feel satisfied that in the region of facts or objects or phenomena, purpose will not be discovered.

Consequently it seems to me that one must look elsewhere. But where to look? Only, I think, where nature itself is threatened and grows confused, where its common and objective properties are themselves lost.

Subjectivity appears where nature gets lost. And it gets lost when the standpoint that distinguishes it from purpose is lost. Nature is not lost in ignorance, that is, in the failure of learning or the deficiency of learning. It is not lost apropos of specific properties of objects, or of ineptitude in dealing with objects, or of peculiar responses to objects. Some people eat birds' nests—a peculiar response if you ask me. But all that can be ascribed to learning, or to some properties of taste buds or gastric juices.

Nature is lost when the processes of learning are themselves stopped. Whoever learns has some view of nature and of his mistakes. There are two places where people can't learn, that is, can't be conditioned. The first—and most familiar to me—is in a philosophic outlook, that is, in some view of nature; the second is in madness. Their common factor is the failure to preserve the distinction between subject and object.

In philosophy the road to the establishment of the subject lies through skepticism. For skepticism means that no belief about nature describes the subject. Nature is lost to the subject because it finds itself in no story of nature. The subject becomes the absolute neutrality, attached to no content and to no form, indifferent to all stories and events. Consequently it has no interest in itself, either, and no way of finding or asserting itself, since any fact or assertion must be relegated to neutrality. The skeptic can't learn or be conditioned. All that leaves him untouched so long as he retains his skepticism and isn't caught in some credulous or self-assertive moment.

In madness, too, nature is lost. Madness obstructs stimuli. Delusion persists in the face of evidence. It is not by offering a history book that one can persuade the madman that he is not Napoleon, that no one has him under suspicion, that his mother isn't going to poison him. Nature as order and as responsibility is lost.

Both learning and conditioning assume the access of nature to the mind or organism. One has to settle for that. One has to settle for nature in both cases or views. Madness is blindness or inaccessibility. Of course, it is more than that. It is more because its inaccessibility is not mere opacity or deficiency. It is a determined and purposed blindness. Something is at stake in the failure of nature to permit "adjustment." So long as the physician stands with nature, he is helpless. So long as he is reasonable, he is locked out and remains ineffective.

If nature ever fails, it ceases to be absolute. In the case of madness, the failure of nature is itself the sign of will or purpose, perhaps "unconscious." But because the failure of nature is attributable to attitude and not to fact, the case for purpose seems to me established. It occurs at least in those situations where learning and conditioning are no longer possible. For these assume nature, that is, objects of logical and causal structure, common to all, or rather, universally operative in ways restricted to their definition or meaning.

Philosophy and madness break down community, that is, nature. Philosophy restores community because it is concerned with the shape of the discontinuous. Madness cannot restore community or nature. Madness is uncontrolled solipsism, just as skepticism is a controlled solipsism. That is the instability of the skeptic; if he is young he may fall in love, or if old into pity. The exhibition of purpose occurs in the failure of nature to live up to its pretensions.

This has to be presented as an appeal to actual experience. One can't hope to make headway in terms of objective knowledge. That is not the universe of discourse in which the argument is valid, because there it is not even meaningful. It would be only through experience, not logic, that the case could be made. And maybe those to whom one appeals have never had a stake in anything, have never been capable of defeat and frustration, have never been troubled by the breakdown of nature, of community, of communication. It is not enough to have seen a philosopher or a madman. One must also have some concern in him, some need to meet, or to restore, some loss of self in the failure to meet or restore. None of that is arguable.

At bottom, if those to whom you appeal don't give a damn about *you,* no argument will avail. That is another form of the suggestion that the common factor in all psychotherapy is the therapist. *He* has reality, and through him all reality gets restored. Our limits as philosophers are all the same as our limits as men. Our persuasiveness is at last only in ourselves.

Of course, the philosopher can act as broker. He can find out what someone values and work from that basis. That is the best way, because indirect and obliterative of self. But one has to know a man in order to find the instance of his love and to lay it before him in its compulsion and terror.

I feel the uselessness of holding to the impersonal when one wants to show the reality of the personal. The environment must be capable of being lost, not just inexpertly met. *The* environment of any man must appear to him as himself, not as content merely, but as the other side of his will. Its integrity is his own, its objectivity the occasion of his purposes. And only some confusion in that environment, which is also a confusion in himself—not a passive mystery, but an active misery—can show the place of purpose. The truth is only what one can put over, and there are some truths that require more than logic to get put over.

iii

Purpose is discovered in the partial breakdown of mechanism. So long as the common-sense world of any given culture remains operative in action, no purpose can be indicated: only training, conditioning, cause, and effect. No value is there seen as the control of action. This is because the value has not been questioned, its relation to the act never explored. Traditionally "healthy" people are on this common-sense level.

Disturbances in common sense may indicate a superior control, or else some unsettlement of control passing into madness. Those situations define the occasions when the values of common sense are brought into question or when they reveal their conflict. The actual world of common sense is confused. As a rule we are content to let this confusion rule, since there are good results to be secured by letting sleeping dogs lie. But sometimes one's religion clashes with one's science, or one's hopes with actual affairs, one's affections with one's duty. In such situations both claims have some standing, but one can't make out their relation, unity, integrity.

Then, and only then, does one encounter purpose, because only then does one find what lies back of purposes, namely the over-all values one needs to assert. There the "id" becomes articulate and needs conscious recognition. These situations are most interesting when the very "superego" becomes accountable to the "id," that is, when the methods of criticism themselves fall under suspicion and need to be affirmed or rejected in a conscious and deliberate way.

This process of criticizing the modes of accepted values (superego, society, culture pattern) is the sole method of establishing the self-determination of one's values and *hence* of discovering *purposes* as the executors of those values.

In the revision of outlooks, that is, of the pattern of nature and of human nature, one comes to oneself. These are the essays we make at self-discovery, of the meaning of the self as integral. History and biography (madness) are the loci of such discoveries. Something was known before Freud. But both are the processes of freedom, and both are secular, temporal, and scientific. Both grow out of experience.

The present world gave birth to psychiatry because the influences that play upon us are so varied and so mighty.

There are many unreconciled versions of nature and of human nature. Madness is more than an individual problem; it is a problem in the definition and revelation of our outlook. Our wills are confused because they have so many authoritative solicitors. I think that much of the case work of psychiatry is oversimplified. Great pressures lie behind "simple" phenomena such as dislike of parents, reconciliation with an ordinary job, war and pacifism, fears and hopes.

Consequently, I feel that psychiatry is one of the avenues of man's freedom. It is not so much that psychiatry is scientific as that it will be a strong element in the establishment of the validity of the inductive and experiential method.

Scientific method is not *presumed* by psychiatry, but is *validated* by the psychiatric disclosure of the humanistic status of the scientific view of nature. Science is not the premise but the *consequent* of psychiatry. As premise one can't even define "mind" or "purpose" out of it. As conclusion, it gets revealed as the order of natural objects with which the mind deals because the mind has asserted the need—its need—of that order for its own integrity.

I don't like the idea of making psychology "scientific." That gives it an environment, and so destroys it. The psychological has no environment. Rather, what comes to be one's environment gets hammered out of the difficulties of experience. But the environment is no datum. When scientists or religionists set up such a prior environment they only make trouble for us and have us ending up in madness. Then, the failure to see that prior environment as one's own creation forces the antagonism of subjectivity to it. And one's subjectivity can't be abandoned. It has claims. Fear and frustration are as much attributable to the tyranny of a frozen environment as to the insurgence of the subjective. Only, that frozen environment has authority. It is the "real" or it is God, or society, or the "good." Then one is headed for trouble. Where environment of any sort is not defined through me there is no reason why I should not go my own way, or do nothing at all.

I suppose I am sensitive on this point because my early

"environment" was ironclad and gave me no chance at all. It has been a bit rough going to see that any "environment" will make the same trouble for anyone who has an ego at all. Any environment not defined through me, and by my consent, is a prison. One gets afraid in prison, sulky, unsociable, and queer. Why not? Many are in such a prison and don't know it. They see no sense in trying to be free, and they make one suffer for the egoism without which one is nothing.

The relation of purpose to the mode of its discovery is important. The mechanists have me on the hip unless I can find a way of discovering purpose. They say one can't find it among objects. They are right in that. Neither do I want to fall back on some subjective inner light. That won't pass. The only way out is to show that the authority of mechanism derives from some ingredient in the integrity of will, that will is defined through some view of common nature and can be understood only in terms of the large shape of nature. For one doesn't react to a tree, but to the view one has of trees. Hindus won't eat meat. The control isn't in the cow but in the way one sees a cow.

15

Libido

i

Libido conveys one's attachment to the sources of pleasure. These are not in the first instance the pleasures of
ecstasy derived from theory but those associated with biology, such as erogenous zones and sexuality.

Pleasure must be absolute or else related to action and
ego. If so related, pleasure becomes precarious. It has to be
worked for and is no longer absolute. As the consequence
of will, pleasure must settle for previous pain or lack and
cannot be undisturbed and constant. This is why a libido
theory, taken as an absolute need, must entail passivity of
will, and so extinction of will.

In so far as one assumes that the condition of living is
active and appetitive, the libido cannot succeed. Its success,
therefore, must be in the region of dream, fantasy, opium,
or alcoholic intoxication. That is why the libido, as instinct,
defines conflict with the ego impulses.

Ego, being will, negates libido as passivity.

However, that opposition, or difference, does not generate the unsatisfactoriness of either. Each could have its
day.

The real difficulty with libido comes from its self-defeat.
Pleasure must be one's own. Yet, that requirement posits
a self or mind having some status apart from the libido.
Libido is not, surely, the enjoyment of objects or accom-

plishments. Nor is it possibly the enjoyment of self. In its pure condition it could not even be narcissistic.

Pleasure or passivity has validity in so far as one must give one's self to action. At the first level, one must accept nature and instinct. One cannot deny nature. The psychiatric libido is always the denial of nature and instinct. It is a passivity that flees action and nature, and hence an unquiet passivity. At the second level, pleasure lies in self-consciousness, in the acceptance of the formal modes of free action, as in art and science.

One should not confuse action with a lack of pleasure. Action can be quite hearty. The passive pleasure of libido is defective in that, avoiding action, it is not really passive just because based on avoidance. He who flees is not free. Libido can be only a deliberate search for the passive pleasure, and, in being deliberate and strained, is haunted by the action it rejects.

To forget oneself in action is a condition at once willful and agreeable. Action is the reality of the self, whereas libido is an abstraction that can propose nothing but a negation. It seeks a content—pleasure—that it can take no steps to secure without inviting care, limitation, and defeat.

ii

The idea of the "libidinous" does not seem to denote an original activity. Activity seems to *become* libidinous. An "egoistic" activity can become libidinous, for example, eating.

The "natural" man seems to be neither egoistic nor libidinous. Such distinctions seem to be based on the relation of an act to the personality or will. (They do not seem to be properties of any instinctive act.)

Libidinous acts are distinctively human. They suggest activity for the sake of gratification, pleasure, or satisfaction, rather than a wholly blind or absorbing activity such as that of animals. The libidinous act puts the personality in the central position of importance.

Asceticism has a common root with the libidinous, namely, both are efforts to define oneself in some independence of natural impulses.

This use of nature for the sake of the personality or self may be called "playfulness." This is not the word I would like, but it has the suggestion of activity that is consciously undertaken for the sake of satisfaction. Playfulness is neither blind instinctive nature, nor is it utilitarian. It suggests "free" activity in which there is enjoyment for the self, and reality for the self. I think it is this note of reality for the self that seems most central.

To view the matter in this way permits a union of the "libido" and the "ego." Instead of taking certain *acts* as egoistic, it seems better to regard egoism as the more general demand that one shall have reality, and that nature and society, at a higher stage, shall not render impossible acts directed to the self's own satisfaction. Ego is essentially, I suggest, a reluctance to submit to control. It is an assertion of value in the very activity that has no ulterior end and no anterior cause. For the egoist, action is the evidence of his entity, but this action must accordingly spring from his own desires and be directed to them alone. Libidinous behavior thus becomes important only as a mode of making the ego real to itself.

Accordingly, I think that the "reversion to the womb" factor in libido has been misunderstood. The basic motive for this escape is egoistic, that is, a demand for the reality of the self. This demand may be misinterpreted as an abdication from all exertion, since exertion is always a reminder of "nature" and, hence, of the limits of one's own ego. But the essential motive of this recession into the passive is the assertion of the self, and of its life, as a value that "natural" impulse frustrates, or natural circumstances restrain. Thus, the pain attendant upon self-assertion is not the *only* condition of such recession. There must be also the demand for the wholly playful status of the ego. One could put up with pain or neglect if one believed these to be parts of a truly playful, self-creative activity. One might even invite pain (masochism).

Religion, art, philosophy, mathematics, science, love, politics, and so on have been presented as valid in themselves. None of the great enterprises seems either the effect of a blind "nature" or the instrument of a remote ideal. All get recommended as having intrinsic value, as if there the self came to rest and was not to be defined through nature or through an absent ideal.

This seems to be the sort of activity that is distinctively human. To be human is to be playful. To be human is, thus, to live in a world of one's own creation, for one's own sake. On the one side, this idea (or demand) leads to depravity; on the other side, to the discoveries of genius. It leads to depravity when the self-contained playfulness yields only fantasy. The worlds of fantasy are always invoked to give reality to the self when nature and circumstances seem to deny that reality. But fantasy is not the reality of the self, because it is lawless and aimless. It is will-less. Action, denied by nature and by circumstance, is not secured in fantasy. Fantasy dissipates the reality of self because it offers no control over a recalcitrant medium. Hence, the self is lost in this *artificial* passivity, quite as much as in the *natural* passivity of instinct. It is this artificial passivity that is depravity, because it is the defeat of the search for the human. It is not a defeat for a human being, but a defeat for the effort to become human, that is, free (playful).

The other side of free playfulness leads to thought in its scientific aspect, that is, to self-controlled activity. The constructions of science are no less "free" than the fantasies of the insane. But this freedom is likewise restraint, control, opposition. Hence it is activity, not passivity. It gives reality to the ego by defining its freedom from nature in terms of its responsibility for the shape of nature, which it has created out of the demands of its own thought.

The meaning of the "abnormal" has never been too clear, and I believe that in these considerations lies a way of joining the decay of insanity and the creativeness of the scientist in the common factor of an egoism that seeks to be in control of activity.

Abnormality is, then, a failure of an essay in humanity. This seems to fit the fact that the disturbances of the mentally ill always suggest the egoist. A good workhorse of a man, the man of habit and faith, faces no mental illness. To be mentally ill one has to have a mind, that is, one has to cherish one's mind for its own sake.

16

Madness

The study of the form of appearance is what I take psychology to be. Nature is not just appearance but appearance in the form of the impersonal.

Classical empiricism has no order at all, that is, no structure, "necessary connection," or criticism. It is neither psychology nor physics, neither subjective nor impersonal, neither appearance nor reality. Such distinctions do not occur in the materials of complete passivity. There one finds neither the normal nor the abnormal—no conflict, no error. Hume and Mill seem to me to have no place for the negative and so none for affirmation either.

I wonder whether one could define psychology without the abnormal. It seems to me that there has always been difficulty over the psychological or nonpsychological status of sense-qualities. The psychological should be disclosed as a property of experience, yet it cannot be disclosed as any item within experience. Nor can it be disclosed as a contrast between experience and something else, leastwise something else that could be known. So, where to look? It would need to be disclosure without content, hence formal. It would need to show the psychological through some sort of collapse, as all formalities get shown.

That collapse is madness. It is not error, since both truth and error can be, and have been, viewed as variations of appearance, as differences in what happens, and so as without authority. Nor is the collapse found in ignorance, since ignorance presumes a systematic limit, and so an ordered infinity that goes beyond data. But it seems that in madness one encounters the loss of the distinction between subject and object, and between appearance and reality— one lives violently, or passively, or in fantasy. One loses nature and self together. Madness is the actuality that shows that order and control cannot be treated as mere ideas or ideals. It is always fugitive, in small ways or large ways. In that sense it is volitional. It is the point at which volition appears in principle as the resolve to maintain particulars, or, as the loss of that resolve.

Nor is the madman an empiricist. He has ceased finding out. Sanity is a "normal" condition and presumes some conflicts overcome. In the absence of the abnormal there can be no norm. What discloses one, discloses the other.

Sometimes the objection to the abnormal rests on determinism rather than on empiricism, on an order that is flawless throughout, unconfused, universal. In nature there is no error, no ignorance, and no conflict. But, then, can nature be found without conflict? And I think that nature needs to be lost in particular ways, that is, through personal confusions that disclose the formal order of the actual. As a student, I was impressed by Plato and Kant; yet such forms seemed in the end arbitrary if made "necessary," and only the phenomenal if left factual, as in Kant.

Universals have to appear in detail, and their neglect must threaten details. They do that when they become a burden. Mad people are troubled and burdened, and not necessarily over creature-comforts. They are maladjusted to environment in principle, not to particulars in the manner of general psychology. The madman is smart enough. Hamlet said that he could tell a hawk from a handsaw provided the wind was southerly. In abnormal psychology, the stimulus-response operations break down. That is why one cannot "get at" the sufferer. That is what makes it all so baffling and uncanny. It is no joke to say that one then sees a ghost. One does indeed. The madman shows the perversion of idealism. He proves, though, that stimuli have a meaning because the naïve view of stimulus no longer operates with him.

Along such lines I would think one could show that "proper" psychologists would indeed speak of the abnormal. Without the collapse and confusion of madness, there is no clue to propriety. Here, the way we think becomes central. Only this way shows the function of criticism in maintaining, not nature, but the distinction between self and nature. Kant showed how to maintain nature, but not how to lose it. The loss must also be part of experience before experience can be self-controlling. This loss occurs as madness, not as error.

Logic, perhaps, deals with the confusion that loses essences, that is, definitions; abnormal psychology deals with the confusions that lose existence, that is, the basis of the distinction between appearance and reality. The psychiatrists are always talking about a sense of "reality," but I fear they mean only common sense. This suggests that the order of essences is enforced only in actuality, that is, in the maintenance of criticism, and so of the difference between privacy and publicity.

In madness, the loss of nature is not intellectual or theoretical or a matter of speculation. There is here a contrast with skepticism, where nature cannot be reached but is kept as a desideratum, just as the self is kept as an actual control. But in madness one seems to have a condition wholly psychic, yet not skeptical. There is in madness no known failure from its own point of view. The abnormal is the loss of criteria. It is the nonfunctioning of very intimately held criteria because of their irreconcilability. It is not the absence of norms. It is not vagrant. It is the disclosure that action requires norms, and that as action grows deliberate and egoistic the need of coherent norms becomes imperative. Action, as critical deeds, must be controlled; the norms or forms do that controlling. But when these norms are themselves confused, then will collapses.

In common sense there are norms, but they are not self-conscious, that is, not affirmed egoistically as will. Norms become our own at the point where they must be asserted as the formal meaning of action. But this cannot be done until action is threatened in principle.

This emphasis on action is also an emphasis on the finite and actual. Neither the opportunist nor the acquiescent formalist becomes mad. It is the person who must give validity to the moment, yet must also have an organized moment. Thus, madness is the systematic frustration of the individual, that is, of the person as an agent, and so as ordered finitude. The idea of ordered finitude (a favorite of mine) gets exhibited in its collapse.

One can see, then, why all monisms take a dim view of pathology. Whether theological or naturalistic, they cannot admit that the individual is the locus of order, or, at least, a factor in all universality. But in madness one makes no mistakes, nor is it to be seen as ordinary willful sin. It is the deeper essay at personal reality. But this personal reality shows also that nature is a function of the integrity of the actual person.

Madness induces fantasy, but without it sobriety is itself without ability to save itself from the charge of dream and phenomenalism. The touchstone is no longer idea but actuality and existence, that is, the self-controlling. Madness, inducing helplessness, is the sign of the condition of freedom where freedom becomes not *what* one wants, but *that* one is actual.

I think that the exploitation of collapse is the nerve of the development.

Sex is surely related to the absoluteness of the actual and finite. People get the idea that sex is a lark. But it turns out to be a restriction. Here lies the deep non-morality of Hollywood, and of successful musical comedy. There is a long record of man's aversion to finitude. There is a finitude without form and prospect; there is another sort that shines with prospect and maintains it. Along that line one uncovers humanism.

The mad are "sick" in no usual sense. There is no local disease here, but a constitutional threat. One cannot even say that something is amiss. It is more than that. More knowledge would not cure it because it does not occur in the absence of knowledge. More knowledge is incidental; but here one seems to deal with the condition of knowledge and of getting more of it. Strictly speaking, one does not know how to cure it. Its cure is always an assertion of the point of view of the therapist, not an assertion of fact, or of what is so in nature. There is a curious use of violence in cures, as in shock-therapy, and also a curious use of personal regard, of interest and delicacy and the restoration of confidence. In any case, there is this confrontation with reality, not with ideas, arguments, facts, or essences. None of that is any good. But the method of cure should be a clue to the nature of the malady.

It is all quite terrible. But I do think that philosophers have not known what to make of madness, and that there is a big opportunity here for new orientations.

17

Management

The free Greek did not equate freedom with vagrancy or anarchy. Action needed control. The four classic virtues present action under control. So there is nothing new in a proposal that action be controlled. Moses proposed it.

There has persisted the view that action *precedes* its control. A brook flows; it is not under control; one builds a dam or a new channel—flood control. To see the control of action in that way is not unusual. People need advice, directing, counseling, "guidance." In various ways we say, "Beatrice Fairfax tells me what to do."

To this view there has long appeared a contrasting claim. It is that action does not take place where there is no concomitant control, but that this is self-control.

It is agreed by all that action needs control. But it has been held that this control is not subsequent to the act, but is *inherent,* that no act occurs in the absence of self-control. The free act is then the inherently controlled act. The expression "free act" becomes a tautology. To act is to be free; and to be free is to be self-controlled, not to be without control.

There is today a readiness to believe that neither of the traditional views of act is acceptable. To be summary: nature appears only as act is excluded. Act is "myth," not an "error" of fact, as if there might be act but that it is not found. Act is not possibly found. This, I believe, is today a powerful persuasion.

The ideal of *knowledge* has long been that we keep out. Any personal participation contaminates knowledge. We are to be passive, receptive, innocent. The prestige of revelation and also of data derive from this persuasion that such knowledge is none of one's own doing. Skeptics see no escape from a private or personal factor. Mystics of certain sorts propose a reality with which we have nothing to do as individual persons.

The knowledge in which we presume to take a hand is illusion. It is not truth. The claim "I see the speaker in what is said" is enough to disqualify the saying. It is a very common ploy. Truth-tellers protest that they are not speaking as themselves. The news reporters protest their innocence. They are not "subjective." Butter would not melt in their mouths. No one may personally appear in what he alleges as his knowledge.

Why not, then, apply the same rule to action? This has been done. The poet invokes the inspiration of the Muses. Prophets and priests act for a god and disavow the act as merely their own. Crusaders march because "God wills it." Such acts, *not* one's own doing as an individual person, are the *best* acts, just as the knowledge with which one has nothing to do is the best knowledge. Let a man once suppose that he acts for himself, and he invites the devil to tempt him with pretty tunes. Where I do not pretend to act for myself, the devil has no leverage. It is the classic claim. Our first parents took the liberty of acting on their own motion instead of resigning to the will of Jehovah. In the true reality there was no place for the personal act. The wise man divests himself of the pretension to act as an autonomous individual. It is a point on which both science and theology agree.

Why, then, should Skinner be regarded as an innovator? Instead of trying to account for Skinner it would appear more in order to account for *those who find him disturbing*. Do they lay claim to autonomy? Who denies that "slums make people" and affirms that "people make slums"? Who repudiates psychiatry with its unconscious controls of action? What scholarly biographer does not "explain" a character in terms of "influences" that account for his temper, beliefs, sayings, acts? It is standard practice. Only a divinity is autonomous. To hold so is also the standard way. For the Christian there is only one autonomous Person.

So, what exactly is the basis of any objection to Skinner? His position seems normal rather than odd. The objectors remind me of the objectors to Berkeley. They do not like Berkeley, but they cannot say why not, especially if they are empiricists believing only the avouch of their own eyes, "the sensible and true avouch," as Hamlet says. I doubt that Dr. Johnson, refuting Berkeley by kicking a stone, would pretend to a divine autonomy in that act. Short of that, however, Berkeley could smile at the doctor's opacity. So, there are mutterings about Skinner, and very likely someone will kick a stone in refutation. Skinner will smile.

A belief in autonomy seems an unlikely basis of objection to a proposal to manage conduct or action. The study of things done—of *res gestae*—is history. I have not found history viewed as a dimension of the "real" world. Theology, physics, psychology have laid claim to disclosing the nature of things, whereas history occupies a limbo neither supernatural, natural, nor psychological. I find that the creation story in *Genesis* rates rather better than the claim that no world can be described or imagined in the absence of a generative past. Dated time, which only acts can generate, is not of the essence. Of course, even clock-time, as in physics, is alien to theological absolutes or to any totality however arrived at. As for psychology, it has no story of a past and lacks even a clock.

So, there is much difficulty in locating an act. A view of "behavior" on assumptions not including autonomy is traditional rather than novel.

Why, then, does a sort of common sense object to behaviorism? Because there are some acts that, although personal, are not occasioned by carrots or sticks or by specific unconscious urges. Such acts are those that are the actual vehicles of order and are so affirmed. The simplest example is in number. To count one does something, one speaks or cuts notches in a stick, one keeps a tally, that is, a tale, that is, a telling. Five fingers and five more make ten, and so do five and five apples. The sum is neutral to specific occasions. Similarly with spatial and temporal measurements. The difference between red and green has to be "told" in some way. So with "here" and "there," with "this" and "that," "yes" and "no," and, of course, many others. Now I propose that common sense identifies itself with such deeds. The average man is not closed to recognizing that much of what he does is "conditioned" by advantage or disadvantage. Parents have always kept a cookie jar. But the counting of cookies is not peculiar to cookies. It is a general command. It is what one does, but it is not a particular doing. One is a counter, measurer, and so forth, in an intimate way. One continues to be. History is made by a few people who persist in the command of numbers, yardsticks, and clocks. The act becomes constitutional. It projects a *world*. Any world, any order, is the *form* of the pure act. Common sense clings to those acts that define and *project* an environment.

I agree with attempts such as Skinner's to show that no act, no autonomy, can be observed as a specific phenomenon or event. On the other side, a totality of any sort, if a *fait accompli,* has always made difficulty for personal autonomy. I am proposing that the act is *itself* the immediacy that generates those distinctions. But this act is a pure functioning, as in the cases cited above. It appears in what I call the midworld, neither in a hidden soul nor in perceived objects, but in functioning objects.

I suggest—rather than extensively argue—that there is no egoism in such formal actualities. One surrenders to numbers and space, to much else. No one can charge that some peculiarity of *mine* appears in such action. It is anonymous. Yet it is also very much myself. At the same time it projects a world, that is, an infinity of order where even accidents are constitutional.

I think myself that the claims of Skinner clarify the issue. Either act is constitutional or else we can have no objection to what Skinner or another may propose by way of control. There can be no "evidence" for autonomy, as if one might, or might not, find such evidence. Autonomy is no *contingency*. It is no *phenomenon*. It is under no *cognitive* limits. One cannot say, "I *know* that I am free." It is no *content of consciousness* that *happens* to appear. It is not a property of any *object*. If one admits to objectivity, the word "free" has *no denotation*. It is excluded from the assumptions of the intellect.

Existence is functioning; functioning is original; its manifestations are utterances—numbers, spaces, words, monuments, all of which are a doing, but not a doing apropos of any specific object or state of affairs. It is a doing that projects an order, a world, a continuum of experience, an *articulated immediacy,* an infinity that is no fact or object but an actuality.

All that leads to the midworld, where appearance and reality meet in the actual. You do have to handle a yardstick, which, however, is no object, but a functioning object.

Men flee presence. They are escapists. Presence means responsible action, a burden, but also an excitement. Psychology defines no presence and so no extension of it into a world. Without such presence there is no meeting ground for argument. The futility of argument has indeed become a tenet of faith. We protest, dissent, make unconditional demands, riot, burn, murder, proclaim "free inquiry." Nothing is sacred, nothing holy. On cognitive premises we become anarchists, and Skinner is *the answer to anarchy,* and his answer, being also intellectual, is a management. All that seems to me quite as it should be, on the premises.

18

History and Case History

Physicians talk of "case history," as do psychiatrists. I hold that case *history* is a confusion.

A medical man keeps a *record*. Neither the patient nor the physician is making history. I go to a medical doctor because I expect him to identify the *sort* of ailment I *happen* to have and then to know what remedy to apply to my sort of disease, in this *case* an application of ice, in that of heat.

Diagnosis is identification of a sort of object or state of affairs. We discover what peculiar condition accounts for an equally peculiar effect. Say your car's engine lacks smoothness; you may think a spark plug fouled, but the mechanic says it's the carburetor. He makes a test to verify his diagnosis. The physician operates in a similar way, takes temperature, pulse, respiration, perhaps sends a specimen to the laboratory or takes an X ray, all to say in the end that he finds symptoms of appendicitis. Your condition is that of a case. You are not unique. Others have had that ailment, and you hope that the doctor has had plenty of experience with that *sort* of disease. When it comes to one's disease one hopes not to be original; one prefers to be a "case" so that the doctor will have some idea about treatment. That is not the way to egotism, but it is the way to medical cure.

You damn a man when you can classify him as a mere sort of thing. No sort of thing is unique. We wish to be unique. If so, one had better not have a medically curable disease. It is humiliating to have the dentist say, "Take two aspirin." He says that to others, to anyone, to people of whom I have a low opinion. He shows me no respect at all. I am a case.

You take some satisfaction in your auto. As is said, it is an "extension" of your personality. All the advertising encourages that attitude. But the garage man tells you that what your car needs is a new spark plug, and he takes one from a box, one of several. You drive out with no more personal distinction than I could command in the old days with my Model A Ford. Not a bit. Of course, the mechanic also has his bedside manner; but actions speak louder than words, and he put a plug into my Ford just as he did in another's Imperial. As Burke observed, "Calamity is a mighty leveler."

Now, what are we to do about this relegation to a mere case? The fact is that we have prided ourselves on scientific achievements, and science has no place for the ego, for egotism, for the original. To satisfy purposes you have to understand what *sort* of object you have to deal with. You get down to cases, as we say. In so far as science is also technology, it is "know-how" in specific cases. Our common detergents contain phosphates; these cause pollution in lakes and rivers; what cleaning agent can avoid the specific effects of such a chemical? What *sort* of thing can wash clothes and not promote the growth of weeds in Lake Erie, monopolizing oxygen and killing off the fish? We deal in cases. Be vaccinated and avoid a case of smallpox, but for measles some other antitoxin is required. Knowledge of cases brings control. It gets results or avoids them.

It seems not too much to say that the rise of such power appears as a chapter in history. It gave us a turn. There was a *Novum Organum,* a new method. The very earth was a case of a gravitational body, to many a shocking disclosure. Science seeks the uniformities that permit us to say that the earth is a case of gravitational order. Mere "data" are absolute. A case never is. It assumes a regularity. That is why I take aspirin for my toothache and get a new spark plug for my car. I do not put an aspirin tablet in the gas tank to cure a sputtering engine: I am not a radical empiricist. I hold with law and order, a very much assailed temper nowadays. Yes, I will have cases. I insist on it. I pay money to doctors because they understand my case and do not prescribe aspirin when my peculiar ailment requires nux vomica.

An early factor in the environment of cases was the atom. The atom has a history. There was, for example, the hypothesis of Avogadro that made a distinction between the atom and the molecule. That a molecule could be composed of several atoms is said to have led to the development of chemistry in the nineteenth century. It opened up procedure. It gave new definition to oxygen and hydrogen. That an element could be diatomic permitted an understanding of many chemical substances and their changes.

Discoveries that modify procedure are historic: everyone who, like me, has had only one course in chemistry, has heard of Avogadro. Now the question: Is Avogardro a case? Is chemistry itself a case? Is history a case? I say not. The atom is not a case within any inclusive genus. It does not "happen," as I happen to catch the grippe. I cannot go to Arizona to avoid atoms or indeed any constitutional factor of experience, any historical factor. Nor can environmental engineers arrange a healthier climate, more convenient or pleasing circumstances, by eliminating atoms, genera and species, yardsticks, clocks, balances, voltmeters, and dictionaries. There is one way out: you can take drugs. If you survive, you are back in the same demanding environment. Having expanded consciousness, you will be wanting your supper.

I should have trouble telling of what the history of chemistry or of America is a case, something that "happens" and could, perhaps, have been avoided. We take steps not to become a case of grippe. We stay out of crowds or keep the children from school. Cigarette smoking may bring on a case of cancer; one quits the habit. It seems awkward to say that geometry or chemistry "happened" to us.

A world without bridge is not impossible, and I hazard that even tennis is more of a diversion than a necessity. The Russians play chess, not bridge. But in all such cases one has to do a bit of counting. Any tennis player can count as high as forty.

A world without smallpox seems not impossible. Why not, then, a world without mathematics, physics, or history? We take pains to perpetuate mathematics and other sciences—an odd thing to do if they were accidental events falling within an environment, like measles or a bad spark plug. Alas, there seems no cure for mathematics, no specific remedy for ridding us of all of this harassing obsession.

You may say that math is a case of learning. If so, you must, I believe, be able to show "learning" in the absence of math, just as you show health in the absence of measles, or even sickness without that malady. Be learned, but omit all numbers, as for example that you eat three times a day or have one wife and live nearer to one neighbor than to the other, who lives twice as far away, fortunately. Even to say one had two eyes and one nose would beg the question. Math and history are not cases of something called learning but rather are learning itself. I do meet people who say that math is a "tool" and language a handy utility—as if they could live without numbers and words as their grandfathers lived without autos, not so well, maybe, although one could argue the point on the premises.

Where I get into really deep trouble is in saying that psychology is not a case of anything but, like math and logic, is a constitutional factor, that it has a history but does not define history any more than it defines physics. There is no more a history in terms of psychological hysteria than in terms of physiological measles. There is no case of which it is an aberration. No difficulty that makes history is psychological. Any such difficulty, like that faced by Avogadro, is posed in terms of structure and procedure.

Psychiatry can tell what you have become (say hysterical, elated, depressed, fantastic) in terms of what you are, or are taken to be, as a matter of fact. The libido, for example, is a fact. Certain modes of satisfying it are facts, a sexual mode perhaps. Of course I consider it odd that anything that "is so" could generate conflict; but passing that by, I would say that in history there are no original "facts" at all. When you first meet the idea that no historian ever tells you what is so you may well be surprised. But how can he? If you want to know what is so about the stars, you ask an astronomer; for the composition of aspirin you ask a chemist; for the medical virtue of aspirin you ask the physician; and so on. And you certainly do not ask a historian about your auto, what kind of gas to use, or where to get a good trade-in. The historian does not tell you what is so.

Well, what has he to say, then? What he says is only that at some dated time—not clock-time—such-and-such stories were told about nature, God, and man. Then he notes a change in the way stories were told. He speaks of what was done, but not of every sort of doing—not of walking over a field, boiling a cabbage, spanking a child, smoking a pipe. On such terms we should all be mentioned in History 1–2 and should charge prejudice if our own acts were passed over. The doing that he reports is a critical doing, one that changed outlook, redirected energies, made men conscious of themselves in a new way. Newton, Avogadro, Darwin did such things. The deeds of history are the critical deeds, those that give a new shape to action itself. Attempt to describe such deeds in terms of theology, physics, or psychology, and they are no longer historical. They become "cases" of some ahistoric and static order. All "theories" of history try to do just that. They want to stand outside of history and view it as an episode, a happening, like measles or a spell of rainy weather.

History deals in acts. Any act is the voice of a design, of a general and universal order. It is only the act that makes history possible, and only history that makes the act possible. It is act itself that has provided the very terms that have called it into question—physical and psychological terms. Those very terms have been hammered out of serious and constitutional difficulties, not accidental discomforts in an otherwise quiet world, not specific discomforts calling for specific remedies while normal life goes on and all our troubles get ascribed to a vague fortune. The historical act shows the difficulty as the very man. He is the same as the difficulty. The historical act declares a world in a constitutional aspect. It is a revelation, a disclosure, a declaration. Psychology describes no act, no originality, no constitutional novelty, no composition.

I am not attacking psychology. On the contrary, I am defending it. To defend it one has to put the psychological in its place among other constitutional and self-defining factors. One has to see its necessity. One has to say that the psychological is no more a "case" of something or other than is mathematics, physics, logic, or the dictionary.

When you see a supposed historian treating the Renaissance or Reformation as a phenomenon to be "explained" on other than purely historical grounds, you can spot the psychologist or sociologist or perhaps the theologian. He makes a "case" of it. Action is not a case of anything. Cases derive from action, not action from cases. The authority of psychology rests on its historical emergence.

One has to remember, too, that history can be discovered only by itself. What else could possibly do so? You do not come upon it by chance or contract a case of it because you did not drink your orange juice regularly.

I have woeful feelings and some indignation when I see that the world and the person may not be historically defined. Well, the indignation is a mistake. No one is to blame for clinging to the "real" world instead of the *actual* world of which the real and the apparent are derivatives. History is secular destiny, and that is a hard idea to present. A good and honest psychiatrist remarked to me that he wished his patients could acquire an "ethical" sense. Apparently "adjustment" is not enough. There is no energy in it, no continuum with the past, a historical and eloquent past.

Of course I can hardly venture in personal safety to say that without the history of philosophy—or philosophy as history—there would be no history at all. Philosophy is pure history and never tells what is so. Nor does one say what is so in terms of philosophic controls. You say what is so in terms of mathematical and physical controls. It is so that Mount Greylock is 3491 feet high or, perhaps, some other amount. Find out on what terms you would call it "false" that Greylock is 3491 feet high and you will have named the special science to which appeal was made in telling what was so, in this case math and physics.

If philosophy were anything other than pure history, its failure to tell anyone what was so would justify the contempt in which it has so often been held. All its words would become nonsense in terms of what is so. In fact, that such is the case has been claimed. "What is it about?" people ask, and there is no answer. But history is not about something else. It is the self-revelatory. There were men not long ago who repeated the old tune about "pseudo-concepts"; A. J. Ayer was one. Russell had a good deal to do with that temper. It is plain that they found the constitutional universal a pseudo-concept because they were pseudo-philosophers. They were not historians. The act, which is the basic historical word, made no appearance in the stream of consciousness or in a postulate set. The success of these men shows the depth of our ahistoric temper. They were all "intellectuals." The intellectual is the outsider not immediately present in his own act. This is the basis of the mistrust of intellectuals on the part of those for whom a past is even vaguely self-identifying. In any past there is something sacred. It is the barbarian who lays his hand on monuments. These intellectuals did not burn the books, but it amounted to that. They were personally annihilative. Russell could not make room for a proper name. What have I done to the past if I treat it as a phenomenon rather than as an actuality continuous with my own?

The pure continuum of history is philosophy, where one never says what is so, but where one develops the ways of telling what is so. Russell wrote a book entitled *Scientific Method in Philosophy*—a plain absurdity, a nullification of history and the self-declarative at one stroke. On that basis there is no present to be maintained, the actuality that generates history.

So, I grasp the nettle and say that the very authority of those who tell us what is so is historical and philosophical. The modes of telling what is so are all historically generated. The physicist and psychologist look around on their terms and find no actuality, and so no history and no philosophy. In consequence the special sciences do not even find themselves. They are not self-conscious, not aware that their very terms make no sense and have no authority apart from the process that forced their discovery. Yes, forced. Any imperative rests on its historical origin, on the self-maintaining actuality that clarifies itself in asserting causes, atoms, and the psychological itself.

If we want reverence, anything sacred and so imperative, we must advance now to history—and I cannot avoid it!—to pure history, which is philosophy. There is the common world, the actual one.

Well, then, a "case" is always described in terms of abstractions, which do not define the present, or, of course, the past. The physician takes your temperature. He takes mine. I have a thermometer in this room. You describe a case in terms that are general, abstract, nonindividual. That is why a "case history" describes a *sort* of event, not a unique one. But history itself is not a case; it is self-declarative and includes the very modes of abstraction by which a case history is recorded. Without philosophy, no history.

19

The Portrait of Man

Does psychology draw the portrait of man? Well, in a painting one can compare the representation with the original. Newspapers sometimes print a portrait, attach a wrong name, and have to make a correction the next day. But in telling what "man" may be, there is no original to which the account may be referred for accuracy. The president always has his portrait painted. He "sits" for the artist. Anyone can tell whether the painter has put more hair on his head than the facts warrant, or whether he has omitted a blemish or shortened his nose. But who sits for the portrait of man? Is it Greek or barbarian, Jew or Gentile, child or adult, male or female?

Not only that, but it seems that the subject never sits long enough for the artist to catch him in one attitude. A moving *object* can be represented in an equation—$S = \frac{1}{2}gt^2$. What equation accurately includes all conditions of even one man, let alone "humanity"? And, anyhow, the changes seem not those of an object, like a stone carried to the top of the tower at Pisa and then sent on its accelerated way.

Of course one can make difficulties apropos of the claim that the artist is no neutral observer. What one of them sees is not what another sees and reports. This variation does not, however, apply to reports of objects. Everybody agrees with Galileo. I have seen students dropping stones from the roof of the physics building. All tell the same story. Why is that? Because all such observation is mediated by instruments, in their case yardsticks and clocks. The object is not observed directly. Treat a man as an object, and similar agreement would result as in measuring the length of his nose, or the rate of his falling from the roof of the physics building. But what is there analogous to yardsticks and clocks with which one tells the story of a man or of humanity? Of course, as I have been saying, the yardstick is not an object. Take away the yardstick, and you have Bishop Berkeley, not Sir Isaac Newton. To know objects you need yardsticks, and yardsticks are not objects analogous to stones dropped from the roof. In short, if no non-objects, then no observation of objects and no physics.

Now a natural science has to proceed through a medium of these artifacts as controls and warrants of observation. I go further and say that these controls *define* an object. What one cannot say is, "There is a stone, let's weigh it," as if the stone appeared as an object quite apart from any account of it in terms of place, size, or weight and then was subsequently examined in those respects. A specific stone can be inspected after it has been noticed, but the region of stones appears only as the correlative of the artifactual non-object. Berkeley wasn't having any stones because he had no mid-world of artifacts. He had only "the divine visual language" and no actual eye with which to apprehend it. He argued that on his terms one lost nothing. True, color and other properties were undisturbed, and what more could one ask? Well, one can ask for objects, for that status. But the price is the non-object, which is also not discovered in Berkeley's "perceptions." The artifactual is not "perceived." What color is a yardstick?

Well, this is rather a long way around the barn, but it helps to explain the *scientific* psychologist's non-humanism. Science needs objects and—*therefore*—it needs instruments to enable it to count and to measure. The absence of instruments with which to describe man then leads to the conclusion that there is no man there to describe. To be an *object* of study one must have those instruments. The two go together. If the portrait of man is to be drawn with the instruments of science, the representation *must* be in centimeters, grams, seconds, and numbers. So if a so-called man moves his arm, or wags his tongue, and if these events are treated as objects, then there is nothing for it but to track them down through nerves and muscles and so to chemistry and physics. Only an obscurantist would deny it. We have an enormous stake in *maintaining* the region of objects. We maintain it by confining our statements to those controls that are the correlative of objects, that is, to the artifactual determinants.

So, where are the humanities? Following the scientist, it is alleged that there are objects, or events among objects, that elude the scientist. There is a soul, or a mind, or an act; an error, virtue, or crime; a good and evil, quite as much as a ten-pound stone. This gets more difficult to defend. On what terms characteristic of objects is one to give an account of the object called a "mind," or of the event called an "act"? The catch is that *science is not a peculiar way of describing certain objects and events, but is the very form of objects.* If the account is not scientific, it is not about objects at all. That has come to be a pretty general feeling. Soul, mind, act, even cause, have come to be viewed not as possible objects that happen not to exist, but as nonsense and "pseudo-concepts." This is more than a prejudice or fashion; it is a consequence of a deep feeling that objects are to be maintained and that the emergence of this object-region is precisely an enormous triumph, the very place where we are at last in some control of statements and outlook. It is getting harder to surrender that hard-won authority. Though it slay us, yet will we trust in it or, at least, mistrust its repudiation.

The attempt to make another object of the subject has failed. Man is not to be portrayed in any way suitable for objects of actual or possible experience. The humanist may then ask, "Well, who wants to draw the portrait as if it were an account, a reproduction, of any object? No," he says, "we deal in subjects, minds, persons—not in things, which are objects." If the humanist speaks in that way, he lacks the basis for claiming any general acceptance. Perhaps he does encounter subjects, minds, egos, but the scientist is not prohibited from turning away, saying that he has never encountered a subject. Let those who say they have talk among themselves but not to him. The scientist has the advantage that even the humanist admits there is talk about objects, and very disciplined and splendid talk, too. And what is more, the humanist is at a loss to propose his own preference *unless* there are objects and scientific lore. Without the region of orderly objects, the very sense of individual selfhood grows indistinct. It was so during the long ages of primitive man.

So the scientist has an advantage. His position is safe, accepted by all, and, ironically, necessary for the humanist himself.

The scientist has another advantage. It is that he has defined an inquiry that permits error. And this capacity for error is inherent in his own statements. He makes mistakes, he can correct them; he can accept a charge of error, he can make such a charge. Consequently he discloses a common world, in that way a decent and disciplined world. He is likely to feel, too, that if it is "mind" that is wanted, why then one need only look at the starry heaven of Copernicus, Galileo, and Newton. What is the poetic portrait of Dante's world without Ptolemy?

The humanist can hardly disparge such claims and sentiments. What more does he want? I think that he wants to appear to himself and to others as an *agent*. When he looks at the starry heavens, he sees no act, nor does he find one in a test tube. So he thinks he must look elsewhere for his act. In so far as we learn *via* machine, we become machine-like in our responses. There is, then, the suggestion that we avoid machinery in order to act. But is not that suicide? How is one to formulate or execute purposes except in terms of regularity in objects? If you want a soft-boiled egg, you need to watch the clock.

The one move we cannot make is to propose a humanism as a foreign addition to science and to the world it has disclosed. Yet such has been a strong tendency. Action, agency, is dependent on the very area in which it seems not to find itself.

Now, instead of attempting to stake out a separate claim for the humanities, why not look for them in science itself? Instead of dreading science, why not embrace it? Because science sees the humanities as incapable of defining scientific purposes and their results, the humanist need not initiate that rejection and allege that science is also outside his interests, or that if he has an interest in science, it is subordinate to his interest in agency.

What I have been proposing is that science is itself a resultant of action. This is not the pragmatism of James or the instrumentalism of Dewey. Their views are psychologically derived. They say that the "true" is found in the success of a purpose. Now, "purpose" is one of those "subjective" forces that the scientist cannot define. Nothing that he says is so illustrates purpose-control. He has swept away such explanations. The starry heavens and the test tube reveal no purposes and no purpose-control of events. But what if one reminds the scientist that his own operations entail not purposes but action? What if one says that the vehicle of action is the yardstick, clock, balance, voltmeter, number, and calculation? To use a yardstick for a purpose is to violate its office. One treasures it and does not use it to prop a window. Liars and sophists use words for a purpose. Embezzlers use numbers in a ledger, or abuse them. Thieves abuse property. Rioters abuse the civic order that has provided their commodities. It is action that establishes the environment in which purposes become possible. And this action occurs through the artifact.

The yardstick, and so forth, is no object. It is not of a color, material, genus, or species. It has no length. It is, rather, the determiner of length. It is not psychological, a content of consciousness, along with all sorts of miscellaneous content. Well, to be more brief: no yardstick, then no physics; no artifact, no physics; no functioning object, no physics; no utterance, no numbers and no anything. If what the humanist wants is the "act," then he has it in the functioning object—and nowhere else. The humanist is not settling for purposes. The most ordinary man has them, and they are a mess, volatile, without command. He wants criticism of purposes. Well, the critic of purpose is the act. It, that critic, is the environment in which purposes are formulated and executed. And that environment is the implication of the artifactual, as space is of the yardstick, time of clocks, logic of the negative word. Psychology must be rewritten. There is no "perception" of the maple tree unless it is *not* an oak tree, and "not" is a word. Without words—artifacts—psychology loses perception and becomes the reaction of rats and pigeons, an event among alleged objects, where no object can be defined, no object-status can be discovered. For that status requires the word.

The humanist should, then, embrace science as a primary locus of action, of functioning. But he needs to see that action operates not from some hidden sanctuary in the ego, but in the public domain, which is not objects but the functioning object. We become skeptics if we see the common and public domain in the unmediated object. There have been many stories. That, in fact, is the root cause of skepticism, as well as of dogma. Both are antihumanist, and for the same reason; neither recognizes the midworld, the artifactual precondition of its own formulation.

The yardstick is an utterance. It is a control. It commands. It projects an infinity, one sort of infinity. But so does logic, for which one must have words. The same applies to numbers. Wherever purposes are arrested by the conditions of formulating and executing them, one has an artifact. Speak a number, and you have to go on to say that there is no last prime number. Say a word, and you must have other words and a dictionary, which is a history book, not a teaching machine. Like a yardstick, the Constitution expresses no purpose and is violated when used for a purpose. It, too, projects a world of action. It aims to state the *form* of action. No more than a yardstick does it serve an ulterior purpose. It launches purposes, it controls them.

When not seen in this way, humanism becomes anarchy.

And some supposed humanists sound like anarchists, as a supposed privacy rejects the establishment and so prefers drugs to decimals and to the world projected by constitutional artifacts. It is fair enough to suspect the humanists and humanitarians of vagrancies. Where is their law? It had better not be merely "inner." And if it is outer, it is not so among objects. Where then? Why, in the utterance, in the midworld, in the functioning artifact and its inherent control, which is also the projection of a world.

The antithesis of scientism is not humanism but historicism. Indeed, science is notably our own and has to fight to win recognition. But the artifacts of science extend the static. They show clock-time, not dated time. The actual requires a date, as does the individual. The world is as much historic as static and physical. And even physics has a past, that is, controls that were inadequate to its own operations. History is constitutional revision, not addition of new information or the correction of errors from an assumed base. It is wholly and entirely concerned with actions, not with objects, not with purposes. It is the revision of outlook in the enlargement or defeat of artifactual controls.

Plato is no part of the humanities if one sees him speaking "truths," as some do. Those truths are not scientific and cannot be so verified. But as a figure whom we must consider but overpass, he belongs to the historic. We owe him our controls because our own emerge from his, although very different.

The humanist must embrace both the scientific and the historic. The question I have tried to answer—sketchily—requires a common factor. It is the functioning object, the locus of action and autonomy. Given the yardstick, what must I then do and say? Vast things, of course. Given the Constitution, what ensues? And so with the Parthenon or Plato or Shakespeare.

The discrimination of modes of utterance and their relation is the philosophical job: What is the structure required by any distinctive utterance, a number, a poem? So, I suggest that the humanist can exploit what the scientist is doing, provided he recognizes that every control word in science is an action word and not the name of any object under the broad blue canopy of heaven.

The portrait of man or of humanity lacks analogy with any representation. An object, and only an object, can be *re*presented. Only an object can be *presented,* that is, put into some relation with other objects. One may see a "model" of a ship, of a building, or of a battlefield. In the exhibition of clothes one hears of "models," where a dress represents what others would see if the spectator were to wear it.

There is no model, no representation of the individual, or of man, or of humanity. One cannot say, "Please point out to me the object that you call an 'individual.' " The soul, mind, spirit is no object either, and so has been regarded as an illusion or worse, namely, nonsense. Such an illusion cannot even be represented as a *possible* object that happens not to exist.

To say "You would do well to become interested in the humanities" is to suggest a possible interest, such as golf, tennis, or aviation. But then the exhortation stumbles because there is no analogy with any specific interest. Advocates of the humanities labor under that grave difficulty. One cannot exhibit as object something called the individual, or man, or the humanities "about" which one then gives an account.

One cannot find *an* individual as one would find *an* apple, that is, an example of a species. If an apple comes to be regarded as anything more than a *specimen* of apple, it becomes a fetish. An apple is merely *an* apple, but an individual or mankind is not merely an instance of a genus of species. One might prefer pears to apples, or one prefers a Baldwin to a Northern Spy and so takes one of that sort from a basket. But an individual person loses that quality so soon as one treats him as a sample.

I think myself that in our time we are quite lost here. I notice, for example, that college students hear talks in sex hygiene where they are informed what to do about *a* man or *a* woman and what to avoid, in view of health and the police. Some like apples, others pears; some Baldwins, others Spies. Pears are juicier than apples, also preferable if one's teeth are sensitive. So, select one of those fruits that best meet one's purposes, remembering, too, that apples keep better than pears and can be used in pies when they lose their perfection. The learner is here addressed as *a* male, or as *a* female, as a sample. So, of course, he can only encounter other samples. Suppose you resist being treated as a sample; then you come under suspicion as a vagrant, or else as an obscurantist if you make a point of your dislike of being a sample.

If there is to be no portrait of man, or of the individual, what does one do as evidence that one has recognized man and individuals? To modify Plato, what is it that is always becoming and never is the same? I answer that it is utterance. The English language is always becoming. The Constitution is always reinterpreted. History is always being rewritten. Any historic individual needs a new biography, and what he said, as contained in an authorized edition, gets restated in every new epoch. The central category here is the utterance, the artifact as expression, the symbol, which is not a representation but an interpretation. Humanistic studies require the vehicle, the actual word— the poem, song, building, ceremony, ritual, discourse. The seven liberal arts are all discursive, and all are based on the sort of control enforced by some utterance. In those arts you do not "react" erroneously, you *say* it incoherently.

To lists of categories I have proposed two additions: (1) the accidental, (2) the midworld of utterance. That is why I look for the humanities in discourse itself. The real, the apparent, the ideal, the useful are the categories of the non-humanist. Humanism deals in the actual, in the present as formal utterance, and so joins the career of utterance in history. So, I am not mentioning the actual as a smart idea but as an ontological factor. There is no portrait of the actual, no model, no representation, no talk "about" it, as if it were a peculiar object or content of consciousness.

The acknowledgment of the actual is also the recognition of the individual. He is *re*cognized, not cognized. He produces a *re*vision, not a vision. Treat a man as an object, and he arouses no question of one's own identity. See him as a person, and one's own acts and utterances undergo change of control. This man speaks like a scientist, and I do not; what would I have to change in myself to deal with him? And why deal with him at all unless I were somehow vaguely allied with his ways? Another is a poet, a queer fellow too, and what he has to say is not what I can say. Yet, if I so much as say " 'Twas the night before Christmas," I have some alliance and have on my hands the question of what there is about me that finds a vague attraction in a poem or song. What would I have to become in order to write a poem? Here is a well-ordered room, a kitchen, perhaps; one is alerted to one's own qualities, or lack of them. I had that experience in a farmer's kitchen years ago and I had to be very careful.

The humanities are the authority of the moment, of the here-and-now, of the actual. Today that authority is not felt in colleges. Teachers are truth-tellers, or moralizers, or propagandists, or utilitarians. One does not go to class just to hear a discourse. Students want it to be "relevant." To what? To their purposes and desires. Even in literature the teacher "explains" a poet psychologically. He is an object, a resultant of a world not poetically *constituted*. Who says today that the world is as surely historical in form as it is physical? And who says that the physical world is the projection of an artifactual immediacy, of a functioning object, which is never a "real" object nor yet a psychological "appearance"?

This moving scene in which we participate has no representation, no portrait made of a sitter, no model. It is the actual, not the real or the apparent or the ideal. It is not phenomenon, not noumenon. Those words are also words and live only in their career.

Ordinarily we use words for a purpose, and that, too, is essential. But the humanities are just talk and *for that reason* are the controls of any world treated as object.

The word must be its own warrant, and that is hard to bring off. So, rather crudely, I grow insistent on the ontological status of the articulate immediacy. Where one has it, one has the humanities. I can see the attraction of song for the poet and why Homer is a sort of magician. But so was Plato, as events prove, only Plato never gave his own utterance an ontological force. His very discussion of the "right" word is a humanistic utterance, in spite of his uncertainty.

The business of a philosopher is to revise the constitution. Well, I propose some constitutional revision. That is not the same as proposing errors. We control the immediate, not the supposed objective world. Cicero has an interesting expansion of the importance of the "appropriate" *occasio* in *De Officiis*. Why would he have fussed with the importance of the moment? Perhaps it was because he was an orator and rhetorician. He felt some authority in utterance.

20

Knowing Other Minds

i. How Do We Know Other Minds?

(1) *Not by physical properties* such as color, temperature, sound; or shape, position, speed, acceleration. Nor by combinations of colors, temperatures, etc. (Such combinations give us objects in *our own* world.) Nor by laws of such combinations of colors, etc. (For such laws describe the domain of physics.)

(2) *Not by physical response.* The stimulus-response situation deals only with mechanism. The other mind is not a stimulus of that sort. The stimulus-response situation cannot give one one's own mind, let alone another's. A finger may be withdrawn from a hot stove, but not from a hot mind!

The stimulus-response situation, being scientific, yields only general or *universal laws* and not *individuality*. Yet another mind could only be an individual, and its activities unique.

Social psychology cannot be carried out in terms of the stimulus-response methods. There is no stimulus and no response with physical analogies in social consciousness.

(3) Not by the application of any of the *categories of physical science,* such as space, time, cause, quality, quantity. Minds are not so defined or determined. Physics is not psychology. These categories give us uniformities, universal laws, not individuals; they omit all the psychological peculiarities.

(4) Not by the methods of physical science, nor by observation and experiment as practiced in science with the senses, instruments, and objects.

ii. The Argument by Analogy

Analogy is an inductive process, an empirical process, an *a posteriori* process. The argument is based on the inference from physical reactions of bodies other than one's own to minds other than one's own. Hence it makes the *assumption* of other *individual bodies;* this is a fallacy.

The general type of analogy is

A has *B* and *C*.

M has *B* and hence also has *C*.

Note the *externality of A, B, C,* and *M* to each other and the absence of *necessary connections* between them. The connection of *one's own* mind and one's own body must then also be empirical, a conjunction *subsequent* to the identification of each.

The analogy might be of some value if it could be stated. *It cannot be stated.* Consider:

Case One:

Bodily condition / consciousness / myself.

Bodily condition / consciousness / therefore your self.

The second bodily condition can be noted, but not the second consciousness as an *object,* and hence the inference is not one of analogy, which *must identify its constituents separately.* We cannot find *four independent* terms in order to proceed to the conclusion. Consider:

Case Two:

Body *A* / condition of body / mind (I).

Body *B* / condition of body / therefore mind (you).

This argument fails to present the *distinction* between the two minds. Yet another mind is not a *case* of mind but an *individual,* and it cannot be found as a mind *except in its individuality.* Such individuality, without which the argument is meaningless, *cannot be provided by analogy.*

Analogy proves *similarity* not *diversity*. The reason for this is clear. Consider a correct analogy:

John Doe / Exeter / good student.

Richard Roe / Exeter / therefore good student.

In this case the property of being a good student is identical. It does not distinguish, but gives a *common* property. In general, inductive and empirical methods yield *only universals* and not individuals. It is very important to note that another mind is not a *sort* of thing, a type or universal property, but something unique, and not to be obtained until that uniqueness is obtained. This result an analogy cannot attain, nor could *any other inductive process* attain it.

The argument from analogy cannot be stated without the dogmatic assumption that the bodies involved are *other* than *the self* that *notes* them, and that they are *more* than its idea.

If the two bodies are *only one's idea* and only within the self as part of its experience, their conjunction with the two selves would be only the *conjunction of two ideas* and would not yield another mind.

The argument accordingly assumes the possibility of what is *more than merely one's own idea* in a strictly *solipsistic* starting point, an assumption that is probably false. In general, the argument assumes that *objectivity* and *nature* are significant from a solipsistic point of view, and that the distinction between *mere idea* and *object* is possible from that standpoint. The first body *may* be only a part of the self. *All* bodies *may* be only that. And if they are not, what is the self with which the body enters into conjunction? Thus the argument assumes also *a self other than its content,* that is, other than nature, with which it makes *accidental* contact.

Summary: The argument assumes

(1) Bodies other than self

(2) Self other than bodies

The argument by analogy gives us only what is *identical* in selves, not what differs in *two* selves.

The argument limits the knowledge of other selves to analogies with one's own body; yet one commonly is unaware of such attitudes, especially in the more emotional conditions of mind.

iii. We Know Other Minds Reflectively

If other minds are *not content* of our minds (which is nature), they must be part of its *form,* that is, part of its meaning or *essence.*

What is not understood as content must be understood as *form* if understood at all. Words can get significance *only in those two ways:* as form *or* as content; as objects *or* as their order; as *parts or* as *whole.* What is formal is descriptive of the *whole;* what is *specific* is descriptive of content. What is formal is original, presumed, ontological, immediate, and philosophical. What is formal is categorical, compulsory, and free. What is formal must be *immediate,* since it cannot be empirical content, accidental datum.

Other selves as accidental datum would *not* be essential to self. Hence they would fall back into content. But the only intelligible content is nature, and selves are not found there because not described by its categories.

Other selves must be recognized to be *the same as our own,* that is, they must have the same character as selves.

Our own self is *a world of experience.* One need not deny here that it is a substance. We are concerned with what the term "I" denotes and, hence, with some aspect of *experience.* We are not concerned with some *entity* in the background of experience, but unknown. Were *oneself* not some *feature of one's experience,* other selves would be equally meaningless in discourse.

Our "self" is a world of experience that *knows itself.*

The self known to itself is not an *object* for itself after the analogy of natural objects. In that region one observes *things,* not selves; content of self, not the mind possessing that very content.

Self-knowledge must be *formal* if it is not the knowledge of content. But the self has no form except that of its world taken as a whole. Form is meaningless apart from content;

but the self has no other content than nature. Hence the self as form is identical with the form of a world of experience, that is, of nature. *Hence another self is another such world of experience* identical with one's own in all essentials. Its otherness refers only to its different *content.* The other self is never absolutely different from one's own. To be a self it must have the same essential *formal* constitution, the same mode of operation, the same processes in so far as one assigns such processes to one's *own* self. To be recognized as other it must also possess the same *content,* at least in part. Completely different content abolishes a meeting ground or mode of contact. While no object in nature is a self, and while no law of physics is psychological, yet there is no way of knowing other minds *except through the objects of nature;* that is, no way of becoming aware of them, save through nature, is possible. But while the road leads through nature, it is through nature as a *whole,* not through its parts.

There are four possible relations of form and content, where they are regarded as varying from one self to another

(1) Content *A* Form *A*

(2) Content *A* Form *B*

(3) Content *B* Form *A*

(4) Content *B* Form *B*

If *A* equals one's own, and *B* another's, which combinations are possible and impossible?

(2) is clearly impossible.

(4) is clearly impossible.

(1) is clearly possible.

(3) is not possible.

iv. Reflection Upon Self Becomes Possible Only Through Other Minds

The distinction between a self and its world, between self and not-self cannot occur in solipsism. Solipsism can claim only the content, the data, of experience. But *one's self is no datum* and would not appear *within* the phenomena. And if it did, the problem would then be to find the subject of *that* perception, an eternal regressus. The objectification of self can occur only in the *objectification of nature,* the only region in which the self, as other than content, can be found. But the self, found in nature, will not be found as an object there, but as its order, *its essential form.* Self will, accordingly, be found only in conjunction with not-self. *The not-self is not nature.* As a panorama of qualities, data, objects, etc., nature offers no escape from unreflective solipsism. For the solipsist cannot escape from himself via the *only* material he has. On the contrary, it is the fact that this material is all that he has that establishes his solitude. Yet it is not really even solitude, since there is no self in the picture, *not even his own.* *The not-self can only be another self.* Only in that way can *self-consciousness* be found. Only in that way can nature become opposed to self. Nature is more than one's own idea only because it is *another's idea also.* This is the *impersonality* of nature, namely its *neutrality* to many minds, but not its *indifference* to mind as such.

v. The Reflective Knowledge of Other Minds

Reflection reaches other minds through the meaning of the individual object, as individual, not as peculiar content. The individual feature of an object, its "thisness," is not a physical feature. It is a feature of order only.

Uniqueness is found only *from the standpoint of the unique,* not as a collection of universals. The standpoint of the unique is the totality of a world of experience, *a self.* In that self the unique gets *oriented* in time, memory, space, etc. This orientation is always dynamic. *The concept of the unique is the concept of an element in a dynamic and reflective order. The unique is a constituent of an organism, never of a mechanism.* The unique is a moment in a process of orientation.

This uniqueness is possible because of the *unique order* in which it is placed, and is unique only within that order. The interaction of bodies or objects viewed as individual is the locus of *mind*. The order of the unique is mental. Objects as unique *do not interact in terms of scientific concepts*. The concepts of science describe the common features of unique objects.

The uniqueness of an object is the uniqueness of its order and derives only from that. The *whole order* or *world* in which it occurs must be unique in order that its *parts* may be so. The uniqueness of an object is the uniqueness of the *point of view* within which it is oriented.

That point of view is a self.

Without other points of view, one's own would not be peculiar or unique. It would not be unique because not conscious of its peculiarity, that is, of itself.

Its peculiarity exists only as *self-consciousness*. It is not possible to define it as an initial datum and then, in the second place, to ask whether one has it. Its *"esse est percepi,"* and it has no other meaning.

It is not the case that the categories, *taken abstractly*, individuate. Space, for example, is not an actual *location* except from the standpoint of a whole self or world of experience.

It is exactly that *wholeness* of one's own self or world that gets no *boundaries* or meaning in isolation. Oneself is not an absolute whole, but a relative whole. It should be closely noted that the attempt to make oneself absolute destroys the *meaning* of the first personal pronoun, and that no orientation occurs in such an absolute, not even space and time, which as *actual location* involve a point of view—and that is always finite and relative.

Further, there is no point of view without self-consciousness and, hence, limitation of self. What limits a self is only a self.

An absolute whole offers no point of view and, hence, *no peculiarities*. From an absolute point of view there are no individuals and, hence, no individual objects.

Thus, one finds objects only through the *self*, through the *wholeness* of the self, through a *peculiar* self, through a *limited* and bounded self, through the *society* of selves.

Nature, as containing objects, is, therefore, only possible socially. Society becomes an *absolute*.

vi. Some Corollaries

COROLLARY: It appears that *communication is necessary* to a self. To be a self is to communicate. To have an objective nature is to communicate. That is the *metaphysical* basis of James's observation about human beings. Our aversion to solitude is not merely a queer psychological fact.

COROLLARY: Since we know other minds only as wholes, communication always involves such wholes. For that reason other persons do not come as isolated ideas, but as points of view in which ideas are found. The idea of another mind is another's idea and is understood as such only as we orient it in another's world. Indeed, the very meaning of an idea requires such an orientation. An idea not my own demands a world not my own as its condition. Isolated ideas are not ideas at all.

COROLLARY: Communication leaves the mark of each self upon the other, not as a new element *within* experience but as an *alteration of the self* as a whole, a transformation of the point of view. That is the real social response. This alteration affects the play of our interest, attention, and appreciation. Communication does not make the content of nature different in qualities or laws. It only enlarges one's concern with such qualities and laws.

COROLLARY: Hence a meeting of minds is a process of *reformation*. Hence it is a difficult and humbling process, demanding great effort, self-scrutiny, plasticity, and courage. The fear of new ideas is basically the fear of *self-renunciation*, for such reformation is the essence of disinterestedness. Only society can make this possible. Even logical disinterestedness presumes this readiness to lay off the old man. Here all the pride of man is marshaled to oppose innovation.

COROLLARY: Nature is *no longer dead*. In terms of a dead nature, minds *could not meet*. Only in nature can one meet other minds, yet only in a nature identical with their life and activities. Nature secures this property in so far as it deals in concrete objects, that is, objects considered as occurring only as elements in a *whole* of experience, which they reveal and embody.

COROLLARY: Nature thus becomes animated, but not animistic. Animism puts mind into the parts of nature. Such a view leads to magic and wizardry.

COROLLARY: Nature as the order of mind exhibits purpose. Nature has no purpose and fulfills none. Nature is understood only as the embodiment of purposes, namely as the order of minds and wills. The revelation of minds is only in their activity, that is, in their power to create new arrangements of nature. Hence also the conflict of purpose and cause is resolved. They are not *opposed* agencies battling for control over the progress of events.

Purpose operates through the acceptance of causal order and natural law. Purpose does not alter the causal character of objects. It *requires* causal order. Causal laws require objects as their seat. Cause determines no concrete event but only *general* events. Cause does not describe a *blind* sequence of events, a *deterministic* sequence of events. It does not determine events at all. If *events* are possible causally, then purpose can get no foothold. It could only *interfere* with their natural order.

Objects, indeed, become significant objects only through *activity* and *exploration*. One does not have them apart from the activity that *defines* them. They are a dynamic concept. *Their being is their being found or made.* It is important to emphasize that *if there are objects in advance of purpose and mind,* no reconciliation of purpose and cause is possible. Purpose must be found in the premises of causal order if it is not to be ruled out in the sequel. *Given* objects and cause and no purpose, the latter can never enter the picture. It must enter as part of the *meaning* of nature *or not at all.* A world of experience is thus a world of active exploration. The exploration cannot be *secondary to the world* if purpose is to have a place. What precedes exploration attempts to show the meaninglessness of a world without such pur-

pose and exploration. And if purpose is a *philosophic* and
not a *magical* concept, it must be part of the definition of
objects, a concept of universal incidence and not a secondary fact introduced into a world already described in
strictly intellectual pattern. It cannot supervene upon content, any more than space, time, or cause can. It must be
essential and integral.

COROLLARY: Nature is hereby shown to be *public*. Its
publicity is no mystery but its essence. Its publicity is no
secondary and imposed accident. If nature were not defined
by its publicity, no proof of it could ever be given. At most
it would remain an accident. Both its form and its content
would elude the claim of community. If its publicity is other
than its reality, there would not even be a way of proving
its objectivity and reality. Hence our attitude toward nature
enters the picture of our morality. Nature is essentially
communal, essentially the property of all, because the being
of all.

COROLLARY: All *ideals* thus enter into the picture of reality. All the categories lose their meaning in isolation, for
they all apply only to nature; but they all achieve their
impersonal validity through society. They are not mine,
because they describe a *common* region. They are meaningless apart from their incidence upon the *concrete individual-
ized object*. Logic itself describes no solitary realm. It has a
community of objects as its condition, because it has objects
as its condition. Morality thus enters logic. Logic and truth
become part of our *duty* and *only for this reason*. Ideals are
not, accordingly, remote from actuality but its whole
meaning as actuality. Hence also, emotion is as ontological
as any other category. Here is its significance in the *struggle*
to maintain ourselves and our world. For such a process of
orientation offers incessant challenge and hazard.

   *It must be an axiom of this discussion that if any part of nature
or reality can be described in independence of the social concept,
our result is false.*

21

A Selection of Paragraphs

i. Adjustment

The cult of adjustment to the environment is absurd. In the end all men are mortal, and death mocks the fevers of adjustment. The cult of adaptation may celebrate its emancipation from the absolute, but it falls victim to the inconsequence of the particular endeavor in the certain obliteration of death. The well-adjusted person can tolerate no general problems, whether of time or eternity. All disturbances of thought that do not apply to specific adjustments and specific satisfactions become meaningless, wasteful, and even mad. The outcome of "adjustment" made absolute is systematic obscurantism.

ii. Knowing as a Mode of Change

There have been many efforts made to treat "knowing" as if it were some mode of change in objects. Thus one says, "This is a rat, and this is a maze, and this is a piece of cheese; let us observe what happens to rat, maze, and cheese." Then one is likely to conclude that the rat *finds* its way to cheese and that this conjunction is a case of knowing. Here is an apparent report.

Why, however, is this report, if a report of objects, called "knowing"? If one says that *some* changes among objects are "knowing," what leads one to that statement? Is the word "knowing" simply assigned to such changes? Is this like saying that "boiling" means the change of water into a gas, and that this gas is called "steam"? Or, does one have any prior ideas about "knowing" so that one would not look for "knowing" in the changes of the object called water, but only in the object called rat? Is there any *restriction* placed upon the locus of the knowing situation? If so, the question of the rat becomes "What do rats know?" rather than the question "How does the object called rat change where there is a maze and cheese?"

iii. Civilization and Its Discontents

I suppose I grew up in the doctrine and belief that the natural man was checked in his passions by truth, or law, or ideals. On the one side, raw nature; on the other, spirituality of one sort or another. Civilization was then the tempering or restraint of nature, but civilization was itself suspect because it was not sufficiently apart from nature and closer to the ideal. Well, now I say that this contrast is only the source of *conflict*. Freud himself brought in the superego. It is in the artifact—the "midworld," as I call it—that the conflict is resolved. I do not find that Freud had that idea. Civilization is not the restraint on nature; that is the role of ideas in the abstract. Civilization needs nature and impulse, and gives them form. Whatever release there is comes through the region of artifacts, that is, through language, which is both action and discipline and self-discipline. It is the one region where one is "safe." The two dangers of nature and ideals are unsafe because they do not rest on the artifact, the one being supposedly inferior, the other superior. I think that the sense of the dilemma of Freud, that there can be no health, comes from his failure—as I see it—to find a systematic place for the artifact, that is, for civilization, for Florence, Rome, and Athens.

iv. Is Abnormality Accidental?

There are many who do not know the difference between a definition and an accidental quality. They want to treat abnormality as an accidental quality, where "mind" or "personality" is defined somehow apart from the abnormal. Then, of course, they suppose that abnormality can be statistically related to the total of previously defined minds or previously discovered minds.

One wonders, then, whether the same holds true in general psychology, whether, for example, one can ask if "memory" merely happens to be a property of mind, or forms a factor in the structure of mind. Or whether odd and even are just accidental aspects of numbers, or planes an aspect of space, where odd, even, and planes merely happen to turn up among numbers and spaces.

Then, too, in connection with the curve of distribution, where the abnormal is the statistically unusual, the same problem of definition occurs. One can draw a curve only where the quality to be studied has been previously identified. The abnormal can't be assumed to be known in advance of the curve, provided the curve is to reveal its meaning. The abnormal can't both be identified before the curve is drawn and then identified through the curve. Here, too, the question of the relation of mind to both normal and abnormal is the central problem. Is mind to be identified in neutrality to that distinction? If so, then one can tabulate the frequency of minds that are normal and minds that are abnormal. But what is the story of mind neutral to that difference? Can that story be told? Or is mind always discovered and defined through the dislocations of conflict, through some systematic maladjustment? Is mind discovered only as the locus of the maladjusted, and as the sole locus?

Mind without maladjustment is certainly unself-conscious. It is not known as mind, as inwardness, as separate from its objects. One can't have both mind and a denial of the maladjusted.

v. History as Therapy

Did you ever hear of a psychiatrist who advised the study of history as the way back to the "real"? I never did. And I depose and say that therein lies a systematic failure in Freud. There is no madness in terms of the "real" world construed as a datum.

vi. Recognition

As one considers one's satisfactions, does one take pleasure in Socrates or Lincoln? And even if we disparage such feelings because of Newton and Freud, still there was Newton and there was Freud, also presences and authoritative.

I come then to the idea that one's first sense of the actual occurs in this recognition of persons in whom we find satisfaction of some sort. There, in some presence, one finds both oneself and one's world.

Still, that is not quite enough. The actual remains unconvincing unless in *one's own life* one has had occasions of satisfaction, so that looking back one is not forever disqualifying what one had said or done or felt. To most persons, others are of no account in their personal past. No experience escapes criticism and patronage. No actuality can find a warrant for such as have not in themselves, in their own lives and encounters, some declarative and revelatory experience. To put it rather simply: We must have had an unquestioned and self-defining satisfaction. Our past is necessary for the validation of a present. Psychology presents nothing past that validates, or invalidates, one's present.

One reaches the point of no argument, not in a timeless axiom, but in a past deed or experience that has been organizing and is not now to be questioned without a collapse of all control and of identity.

vii. Man as Rational Animal

If it is said that man is a rational animal, one requires some disclosure of such rationality. What is that disclosure?

To say "Man is a rational animal" is *not* to ascribe a quality taken as accidental, as in "Man is a long-lived animal," where there is found (1) man and (2) longevity.

So, the quality of rational is essential or constitutional: no rationality, then no man.

The quality "rational" is, then, inseparable from man. Nothing a man *appeared* to be in terms of some environment—his color, height, physiology, chemistry, biological species—could serve to permit his being called rational. Nothing a man *did in terms of an environment* would show him rational—food finding, walking, swimming.

As rationality is inseparable from man, so must be its manifestations and the *vehicle* of its manifestation.

So, what is the vehicle of rationality? Of this self-containment, self-expression, self-criticism? That man is *not* rational (perhaps not irrational either) is a claim made because the account given of man has not been given as a self-containment. Man's rationality has been alleged apropos of what was *not* identical with him, as when he discovered "truth" about nature or made "adjustment" to the environment, or manufactured tools for various purposes. But to call man rational has not been the same as calling him intelligently cognitive. Animals not regarded as rational have been called "intelligent." Even "tools" that make for specific results are not confined to man. Put an alleged man *inside any environment* and he will not be able to show his rationality in so far as it is described in any environmental terms or relations whatsoever.

Rationality and the mode and *vehicle* of its exhibition must be the same. And they must be immediate to man and identical with him.

Now, then, *what is the vehicle* of self-disclosure? For that is what the claim to rationality *must* offer. I claim that it is utterance, the midworld. It is this vehicle alone that permits the distinction of individual and nature.

What is required for rationality is not an empirical or mysterious attribute of man as "animal," the attribute of rationality. What is required is a vehicle that is quite distinct from any statement whatever—any quality whatever—made "about" man. That vehicle, which is neither ego nor environment but the very condition of that distinction, and of *all* formal and organizational distinctions, is *utterance*. There is the evidence and vehicle of all self-revelation *and* of the world as well.

It is only a self-generated and self-policing utterance that appears as the actuality of reason. There alone is form. If reason is no "appearance," it must either disappear or else occur in some other way. That way is utterance, which is actuality and the locus of all formal distinctions. Rationality is the control of form, and that is self-control.

A consideration: If one says (1) "Man is a being among others" (mineral, vegetable, etc.), and if one says (2) "Man is an animal" (not a vegetable or mineral), then one cannot *add* that man, the animal, is *also* rational.

Man cannot be rational as *object,* or as *attribute* of object, for example, "animal."

Rationality can be no quality discovered in *any prior state of affairs whatsoever.* "Rational" is no predicate of a subject of discourse.

viii. Unwanted Experience

Neither an object called nature, nor one called society, strikes back at an alleged person who is external to both.

A belief that nature does not strike, but that God or spirits or demons do has been common. The point is that a privately unwanted experience is no evidence that nature, rather than God, has affected me. Skeptics had their aches but were in no position to attribute them either to nature or to God, or to anything.

Except as nature is the *form of action when impersonal,* one cannot say that nature is lawful, or that its laws operate upon an individual. If the "laws of nature" were other than the form of action, they could not be known as law. Nor would it be possible for them to have any effect on the person not already allied with nature.

Society, like nature, had no original objectification. An objectified society is a result of egoism. In actuality, we are as close to society as to nature. Society is the *form of action when personal*. This structure is no more at one's discretion than is the order of nature. Just as we discover nature through a mode of *pure* action, so too do we discover society in our individuality—in personal pronouns, proper names, speech, custom, and so forth.

Both nature and society are made known by the confusions of a failure to be identified with their form. Society acts upon a breach of its conditions as also does nature act upon us through what we have ourselves been doing.

Society does not *punish* an individual external to it.

ix. Past and Present

Our strongest desires do not endure in a merely positive form. A great deal of psychology has employed the "pleasure-pain" or the "appetition-aversion" couple as the explanation of behavior. But enduring tenacious effort has nothing to do with either carrots or sticks. Psychological explanations arc valid for purposes, not for will. They leave action accidental, the resultant of native urges or of irritable protoplasm as these encounter environmental promise or threat. The general success of psychological explanation of action bears witness to the absence of recognized constitutional controls of experience. It is a waste of time to talk about history when the assumed framework of an alleged act is taken to be some version of "stimulus-response," however much that frame of reference may be complicated by supporting studs and rafters.

Nothing in the world can make one aware of nature. One of the historic contributions of the rise of abnormal psychology lies in its terrible disclosure that the sense of nature is a consequence of one's own composure, and not of visual or auditory stimuli operating upon an innocent, if raw, desire. The appalling presence of a mind incapable of maintaining the distinction between self and nature through the vehicle of particulars marks the failure to grasp nature as an idea. If empiricists want to establish the authority of particulars, they would be well advised to abandon red patches and atomic facts and consider the dreadful instances of minds for which the particular has lost a constitutional authority. Nature is an idea and, therefore, a factor of self-consciousness. The man for whom nature is a fact, or a perception, or an object, will not be in a position to understand the idea of history. As an idea, that is, as a constitutional factor of experience, history is a reaction to the views that see in nature either an accidental content of consciousness or an absolute object.

The earliest condition of man shows him as already aware of time and as defining himself in terms of deeds. The idea of history accredits time and adds to its meaning, but the sense of time is older than the recognition of its constitutional status. In his well-known book, *The Ancient City,* Fustel de Coulanges gives a beautifully detailed account of the early individual and his social environment. It is a true history in so far as it tells a story of what people thought about themselves, of how they defined themselves and so the world around them. The keynote of his exposition is in piety, the sentiment of Aeneas looking after his father and carrying his lares and penates to Latium. To be a person meant to have known ancestors and to maintain the undying flame upon the family altar. Slaves and strangers lacked such identity. They owned no burying ground for the dead, performed no rites, lacked the obligations of a descendant, and the anticipations of regard from their posterity. Identity was the actuality of a particular life and of one's own family or tribe. In declining an opportunity to save his life by escaping from prison, Socrates, as late as 399 B.C., voiced an ancient sentiment. For he was the son of Sophroniscus, an Athenian, and Athens was his mother.

To ask whether such views were "true" is like asking whether sweetness is triangular or beauty a mineral. The more we patronize such sentiments, the more we are embarrassed to account for their occurrence in a world that leaves them so absurd, implausible, and superstitious. No man's identity is the consequence of an argument, nor is it changed by argument, where one means a marshaling of facts and inferences. This is not because the facts are false, or the inferences invalid, but because facts derive their prestige from the outlook that accredits them. The Christian is not likely to believe that miracles attended the birth of the Buddha, or that Mohammed ascended to heaven on his horse. Persons are not anonymous. Nor are they found objectively in a time or place like particulars of nature. There is no Athens without Athenians, and what the place meant to its inhabitants is not a corollary of physics but a constituent of their identity. What they were took time to establish.

No person, and no society, exists in the present tense alone. Just as nature as lawful order is unknown apart from the changes of objects, so too is a person undiscoverable apart from his acts. These are an original dimension of his identity. The gentleness and the courage of men, all their civic virtue, inheres in their respect for the processes that take time. One can hire a technician, but not a friend. Our friends see us in our actuality, in our defects and values, and yet for all that take the trouble to say a word. It costs them something, for there is recognition. No doubt such a view can breed sentimentality or a shallow egoism, but then the worst is ever the corruption of the best.

x. Preoccupation with the Psychological

There is a common-sense appeal in the admonition "Let your mind alone." A healthy attention is directed upon objects. There we find nature, God, other persons, a world for our wonder or exploration. Besides, preoccupation with one's own mind results in no practical information. How to make a fire, to build a shelter—to do all that brings convenience, health, safety, power—gets discovered in paying attention to objects, and not to one's mind. It is also such knowledge of objects that permits one to assist other persons in their purposes or needs. Practical morality has no other way of showing itself. Without skill to make a living one cannot support wife and children or demonstrate regard for their welfare. God helps those who help themselves, and, on the same basis, one may be of service to others.

The oracular advice "Know thyself" has the broad effect of turning us away from the practical and moral. But what is there to know about oneself quite apart from particular engagements? Even self-knowledge appears apropos of some capacity. One is a good carpenter or sailor, a good citizen of Athens or Sparta, a poet, a scientist. Whatever mind one has makes its appearance in a knowledge of skills and of objects, in one's competence or incompetence. Have whatever mind you like; but if you require a fire for your comfort or safety, or for that of others, it is necessary to know that a little dry tinder is required to start it. People preoccupied with their own minds are "out of their minds." Therapy consists in restoring occupation and avoiding preoccupation. In terms of the mind itself there is no cure for madness because there is no discovery of it.

One is confronted by a seeming paradox that to have a mind of one's own, and not to be "out of one's mind," is to be occupied with objects, with something that is *not* one's own mind. It is commonly accepted that a person who uses drugs should consult a psychologist for therapy. But our preoccupation with the psychological is itself a *cause* of the psychedelic quest. "Consciousness expansion" was not a recommendation of physicists or of locomotive engineers. It was a term proposed by psychology. To be sure, the psychedelic haze is a way out of disturbance and conflicts. But it is a state of mind that extinguishes self-knowledge along with competence in dealing with objects. In terms of the mind alone it is not possible to say "I am mad" or "You are mad." Sanity is not a condition within the limits of the psychological. That many have not questioned the psychological locus of insanity is an evidence of preoccupation with our own minds.

Very large-scale consequences ensue: child-centered education, permissiveness, entitlement to opinion where no "title" is to be regulative, the charismatic politician, Disneyland and Camelot, the assault on the establishment in any form, the importance of dissent as the evidence of a superiority to any actual mode of self-maintenance. For Hamlet the times were out of joint, but he proposed to set them right. No one can propose that today. We are disjointed, and any proposed jointing—even causality—is assailed as without force, or even presence, in the stream of consciousness. In psychology there are no joinings. The youth culture used the word "happenings" to indicate an unconnected moment. The question "How did you happen to forget?" has no answer within the limits of consciousness alone. Where all rules are off, anything can happen, and whatever happens is no more than another disjoined happening. In terms of happenings the popular song "Don't Fence Me In" is quite appropriate. There are no fences in the stream of consciousness, no banks that confine the stream and mark its place.

The curious but inevitable result has been an increasing reluctance of psychology to deal in consciousness. The reason is a good one: consciousness is no item of consciousness. The consequence is behavioral science. This is the acknowledgment by psychology that consciousness explains nothing that happens. It is indeed to be exorcised, as in physics. That is why it calls itself a science. Nothing in physics is accounted for as a consequence of consciousness.

The negation of physics—that changes are not to be accounted for by the operations of consciousness—is appropriated by behavioral science.

Whereas psychology originated and long continued as a study of mind, it has now abandoned that assumption. This outcome is not, however, merely a capitulation to physics; it is the result of the loss of control within psychology itself. Psychology could not, within its own limits, discover consciousness. It could not say what it was talking about.

Consciousness was jettisoned. It came to be regarded as not empirical, as a hangover from a superstitious age. But that is not the bottom reason for discussing psychology as the study of consciousness. The reason is not that the psychological is a spook, but that it is a chaos.

xi. A Psychological Start

Far from denigrating the psychological I claim it to be necessary and structural. But the authority of the discourse that would say so is generally denied. For the most part philosophers have attempted to escape from the psychological as "mere" appearance. One wants to get rid of it. It is amusing to note the reaction to Berkeley, who proposed, not quite successfully, that we stay in psychology, that "To be is to be perceived." But Berkeley is good medicine for anyone who alleges that from a psychological start one can get to a nonpsychological content of consciousness.

22

*A Selection of Notes**

i. A Mind Is Unique

In psychology we deal with the unique. A mind is unique. So, though we use an observational method, it is not strictly the scientific method. No scientific law deals with something that is unique; all scientific laws are generalities. The summation of universals does not give the unique.

ii. Memory

Every property of a mind describes a function, a relation, not a thing.

Memory is a mental function in which all other mental functions—thinking, imagination, and the rest—are involved.

Memory is not to be defined by the character of the object remembered. Nor is memory to be distinguished from

*This is a selection from the notes taken by M. Holmes Hartshorne, subsequently professor of philosophy and religion at Colgate, on Miller's course in psychology at Williams in 1930–31. This course was, like Miller's other courses, partly original and partly a sort of commentary on the textbook, in this case R. S. Woodworth's *Psychology,* then the leading text in the field. At one point Miller remarked, "He never encounters a mind at all until he gets to page 242." This selection is intended not to give an outline of the course but to indicate Miller's treatment of some topics not covered by the essays in this volume.—ED.

perception or imagination through qualities of the object, or by clearness or vividness.

Memory is not an independent function. It occurs in connection with perception and purpose.

Perception is a reconstruction involving memory material. No meaning is photographic, i.e., a mere reproduction. You cannot put all perceived things in one bag, all memorized things in another, and all imagined things in another.

Memory is an element in the structure of fact. All objects have meaning only through memory. All memory is psychological. Therefore, all objects have meaning only through the psychological.

iii. Facts

A fact is a proposition that fits into a structure. Example: "Today is Christmas." That may be correct one day in the year; it fits into the structure of human experience then. Evidence for a fact is seeing how it fits into the structure of knowledge.

Every object is a theory. One never really explores a desk, a piece of chalk. With certain aspects noticed, one theorizes about it: that the desk has a bottom, the chalk weight, and so on.

An imagined dollar differs from a real dollar not in the attributes of the dollar but only in that one is real and the other imaginary. What makes it real is the way in which it fits into the structure of our experience. The same difference exists between false and true propositions. In short, the difference is in form, not content.

Every rejected fact or proposition is rejected because it cannot be fitted into the structure of our experience.

The study of structure throws no light on experience. A man born deaf cannot ascertain what a sound is like by studying the human ear and all allied organs.

iv. Reflex Theory

The conditioning of a reflex is as primitive as the reflex itself.

There is a set of facts that exists only in our own world of experience and could get no meaning from conditioning. All are concepts of form as against content, for example, space, time, truth, logic, cause, self, other self. These have no sensory content and cannot be learned about in the conditioning manner.

You can't bring direction and consciousness into the reflex theory unless through deception. It is essentially mechanistic; and except by deception, ideas, consciousness, will, direction, cannot be entered. You cannot have more than a curiously involved objective mechanism.

In the theory of the conditioned reflex there could be no enlargement of the mind since there would be no mind. Learning would be an objective reaction or change rather than a subjective acquisition. One who tells the story of the foundations of human nature only in terms of reflexes cannot well understand it; he needs must tell it too in terms of the goals these actual deeds are seeking to fulfill.

You can't acquire goals or ideals. You can learn what goal you want, but you must have it initially.

v. Heredity and Environment

There are two types of heredity:

(1) Heredity subject to determinism. This type of heredity is the type discussed in the textbooks and is always subject to environment. A given attribute is subject to other conditions.

(2) Heredity not subject to determinism (not governed by environment), that is, freedom, self-direction.

How would one know or where would one look for what is not a determined heredity? Nowhere in objective nature—that is, in what is peculiar or local, either physically or psychologically—but in what is essential to a self, in the definition of the self. Not in any accidental or peculiar property of the self, but only in what is self-determined.

vi. Fate and Freedom

Not anything that is objective about me is what is free in me. Where we are peculiar—where we are different from one another—we are victims of fate.

There is one set of facts that is peculiar to us: whatever goes along with mind—the general structure of thought, not what I think. The locus of one's nature is not in local peculiarities, but in the purely structural concept of self. What is common to you and me is not governed by environment.

vii. The Method of Psychology

Most things we study relate to content of experience. In psychology the content would be such things as the conditioned reflex. With that kind of learning we are familiar, but psychology offers more than that: form.

Study of self cannot be done by putting the mind on the table. Your brain is not your mind despite the fact that your mind cannot get away from your brain.

Reflection is knowing oneself. What is the structure of knowledge, of mind? What is that which I call *I?* That is reflection. Reflection is a method of knowledge. Reflection is a knowledge of form (as contrasted with content). Both introspection and observation give knowledge of content.

Content is anything particular.

Grammar is a good example of form, for in it we learn how a sentence is constructed, and it is the same whether the sentence expresses the fact that Columbus discovered America or the fact that John is a good boy.

What you mean by the structure of your thought only

your thought can reveal. That is reflection. When you study logic, you study that way in which you study. Thought as structure, the character of thought, the way it is put together—these reflection brings out.

The kind of fact you get in reflection is not a fact of history. What makes a fact true does not depend on whether it is remembered or not. Reflection brings out facts of structure. The character of the mind can be got at only by the mind scrutinizing itself, only as properties of its own experience, not as external objects.

The structure of the mind is in essence the thinking process. Unless self-study is possible, psychology is impossible.

Reflection is not subjective. It is a study the answers of which are irrelevant to private history. The general type of fact when you are "minding" is the same whether you are born in Connecticut or Paris. Such facts are precisely what they are no matter what your own opinions on the subject may be, what you think about it. If it made any difference whether it was a cat getting fish or a monkey a banana, we would have *"n"* psychologies. The rules of learning apply to typewriting just as to telegraphy. Introspection is reporting your own frame of mind (to yourself, if you are to be very strict, since communication is a form of overt activity). Reflection has to do not with what is accidental to our experience but with what is essential, not with the details but with the structure of our experience. The accidental is what could be otherwise. The essential aspects, the unavoidable aspects of the mind are what makes it a mind. The most important things in life are what we have with us always and little understand.

Reflection explores the structure of the self. Anything not structural to self is found by observation and experiment. What is structural to self is in *all* specific experience and cannot, therefore, be found by experiment. You can experiment only where things are different. Reflection tells what one starts with. Experiment tells what one ends with.

The study of concepts without which science cannot be

conducted is the philosophy of science. Examples of such concepts are number, time, space, quality, necessity, logic, cause.

The study of concepts without which thinking cannot be conducted is psychology.

Any way of looking at reality is an organization.

To be a mind is to be active, to be purposive, to have a goal, to be more than a mechanism (since things would not be as they seem but as they are in a mechanical world). A question implies a world of experience not sure of itself, and that is a mind.

viii. Body and Mind

Body and mind are not separable but are only functions.

It does not seem to me that you can have any sound philosophy that denies either mind or body, nor one that holds them distinct. If one thinks, one must have something to think about. I cannot find a mind that has no content. I shall offer a prize to anyone who can find such a mind in the history of philosophy. Mind has "furniture," called nature. No one can describe a mind without some content. It has no being until it has furniture, and that furniture must be that we call nature.

ix. Purpose

If there is any difference between the living and the dead, the answer is to be found in terms of purpose. If you invent purpose, you have got to start with a situation where there is no purpose. This is not possible. You either know just what purpose is or you do not know it at all. It cannot be an invention or a daydream. It is essential to invention: if you invent something, you have purpose. Purpose is a property of the world considered as a whole, the property of a world able to enlarge itself, to grow, to gain in power.

It is not something *in* your world; it is something you know directly. It gives your world direction of growth. It is to be found only in an aspect of world that makes for fulfillment of your world. Use of such words as *failure* and *success* imply the knowledge of purpose.

One does not have purposes; one is purpose. You are not there to have it until you are it.

Purpose is not *in* your world, is not known through the senses. It is not a thing such as a gold mountain, not an entity. Purpose is a feature of the world: its own law, its essence. You do not come by the concept of purpose; you become self-conscious. It is always with you. It is mysterious because it is the essence of our being, not accidental; because it is of structure, not of content. Anyone who affirms the reality of a world of experience, truth, or error affirms purpose.

You don't wonder *what* purpose is and then *if* it is, but you find it as an essential property and it must be.

A world in which purpose is real is not capable of a purely mechanistic or materialistic interpretation. You cannot find purpose in mechanism. That is rock bottom, I think. An infinitely involved mechanism does not give purpose. You cannot generate from the nonpurposive to purpose.

There is a class of concepts such as memory, space, time, purpose, and so on of which the very idea establishes the reality, first, because they are concepts that cannot be composed from anything else; and, second, because they represent the very structure of the world of experience. They are essential to it.

If purpose is vague, so are number, time, space, quantity, memory, and causation. But there is nothing more certain than purpose.

Purpose is the way we understand the relation of individual to individual.

You can tell why fountain pens make marks on paper; science does this from the standpoint of universals. But to find out why this pen makes this mark on this paper you must consult me. Mechanists attempt to explain this latter from the standpoint of universals, but it cannot be done.

x. The Universal

There is no receptor for the sense of space. You cannot have an organ for a universal property. There is no thing, no object, without space. You would destroy nature if you should destroy space, but not if you should destroy sight or hearing.

Space stands not for a quality but for the order and arrangement of qualities. It is one way in which unity is brought into variety. It is a principle of unity and order.

Space is the concept of the simultaneous. Space is one of the absolutely essential concepts in attempting to know what an object is.

Space is not an accidental feature of our world. It is essential to a world having objects; if you have no objects, you have no things, no nouns, and you are reduced ad absurdum. The idea of an object is the idea of variety and change according to law.